Outrageous
Exceeding the Limits of Usual

Myron Pierce

© Copyright 2013 Myron Pierce

Unless otherwise identified, Scripture quotations are from the New King James Version®. Copyright © 1982 by Thomas Nelson, Inc. Used by permission. All rights reserved.

THE HOLY BIBLE, NEW INTERNATIONAL VERSION®, NIV® Copyright © 1973, 1978, 1984, 2011 by Biblica, Inc.™ Used by permission. All rights reserved worldwide.

Scripture taken from *The Message*. Copyright © 1993, 1994, 1995, 1996, 2000, 2001, 2002. Used by permission of NavPress Publishing Group.

All rights reserved.

ISBN-10: 1481893238
ISBN-13: 978-1481893237

DEDICATION

Dedicated to Kristin, Amillion, Jericho, Judah, and most of all Jesus Christ.
"Now to him who is able to do immeasurably more than all we ask or imagine, according to his power that is at work within us."
-Ephesians 3:20

CONTENTS

	Acknowledgments	i
	Forward	1
	Introduction	P. 3
1	Full Circle	Pg 9
2	Before and After Pictures	Pg 29
3	Dream Sheets and Impossibilities	Pg 35
4	The Point of No Return	Pg 42
5	Faith it Till You Make it	Pg 50
6	Building When Everyone is Laughing	Pg 58
7	Close Calls	Pg 65
8	Stepping Stones	Pg 73
9	Gold Nuggets	Pg 83
10	Exit	Pg 92
11	Transition	Pg 98
12	The Land of Promise	Pg 105

"YOU'RE PURPOSE IS BIGGER THAN YOUR PRISON."

ACKNOWLEDGEMENTS

There is much more to be said. When one door closes another door opens. Months after writing this book God opened up a great and effectual door for me to head to Colorado Springs, Colorado to plant a new church. We are excited to advance God's Kingdom in this way.

There are many people who are responsible for the fruit of this book. Lord knows I would not be here if it wasn't for the grace of God. In addition, my great mentor Ron Dotzler has been a catalyst in my life and I would not be in this position if he didn't not only believe in me, but give me opportunity to lead. Thanks Ron and Twany.

Everyone needs a Josh Dotzler in their life! Thanks for believing in me bro. Without you I don't know where I would be. Better together is more than a phrase it's a way of life, and you've taught me that.

Much props to Bobbie Jo! I remember sitting in my office going over mustering the courage to starting writing my story. She came in, interrupted my thoughts, and created a writing plan for me in less than one hour! You're an amazing leader. Thanks for believing in me!

Abide Network and Bridge Church I love you from the bottom of my heart. All of you who I have not mentioned it's definitely not on purpose. That would take a whole new book. Thank you. Thank you for your words of encouragement and prayers. That includes my good friend Isabel. You are amazing!

I remember connecting with my friend Sheila about this project and one thing led to another – she decided to take this manuscript through the editing process. Sheila, thank you for your time and effort in making this possible.

Finally, I want to say thank you to my beautiful wife. I'm honored that God put us together. He knew that I needed you. He knew that if I was going to become who he created me to be, then I could not do that without you. This has been a long time coming, but I'm eternally grateful that you've stood by me every step of the way.

Thank you for taking the time to read my story. We all have a story. Hopefully, you have been inspired to see a new you, and to allow Jesus to be Lord of your life. If this book has helped you in anyway please feel free to email me at Myron@passioncitychurch.cc

FORWARD

My Zimbabwean brother, Cainos, once told me, "The man with an argument is at the mercy of the man with an experience."

Has someone ever told you something that shifted your whole life? I once heard someone say, "One word from God can change your whole life!" Once those words jumped out of my friend's mouth and parachuted onto the ground of my heart, I became a different man!

We live in a different world that demands different people square their shoulders and say with audacity, "I'm going to make a difference." Not to be cheesy, but I believe in the heart of Michael Jackson's song: "Let's make this world a better place!"

Why did I choose to write this book? I want to make this world a better place! I think that's what God had in mind when He sent Jesus Christ to the earth thousands of years ago! God wanted to make this world a better place, and He did! God's original intent was to reconcile the world back to

Himself, and in so doing; He reignited the human heart to do the impossible!

I wrote this book so that God would use it to catalyze a movement of people who would become alive and awakened to a new way of thinking and acting. This book will challenge you to consider your place in the world! This book will ignite within you a vision to believe that we are not waiting for God, but that God is waiting for us to become radical world changers!

This book is simply a chronicled journey of how I am learning to be outrageous, to exceed the limits of usual. You, too, were created to be *outrageous*!

INTRODUCTION

I recently finished a book by Mark Batterson called *The Circle Maker*. If you have not read this book, you are sinful! Okay, I'm just joking, but this book is a must-read for everyone! In it, Mark talks about this miracle worker named Honi.

During the first century BC, a variety of religious movements and splinter groups developed among the Jews in Judea. Many individuals claimed to be miracle workers in the tradition of Elijah and Elisha, the ancient Jewish prophets. The Talmud provides some examples of such Jewish miracle workers, one of who is Honi, famous for his ability to successfully pray for rain.

On one occasion when God did not send rain well into the winter, Honi drew a circle in the dust, stood inside of it, and informed God that he would not move until it rained. When it began to drizzle, Honi told God that he was not satisfied and expected more rain; it then began to pour. He explained that he wanted a calm rain, at which point the rain calmed to a normal rain.

Before I ever started reading *The Circle Maker*, God was doing something pretty amazing in my heart. As I got up every morning at 4:30 to go to our facility and pray, I started praying and reading *The Circle Maker*! As Mark Batterson dynamically articulated the story of Honi in the context of prayer, it dawned on me that I am a circle maker!

You may already have the insight that you're a circle maker and that God could use you to do something totally amazing! However, as I began to think and pray through this more, I began to draw circles around writing this book. At first, I thought to myself, *It's not the right timing to write a book*. I came up with various reasons why I shouldn't write a book and the list was numerous: one-year-old son, wife pregnant with another son due in June, co-pastoring a new church plant, and the list went on and on!

Deep down, I knew it was time to get started writing this book. I keep a prayer journal so that when I'm in prayer I can chronicle what I'm praying and what God is saying. One morning I wrote down, *I want to write a book*. That's a pretty safe sentence, right? It wasn't a full circle. I didn't put a title, subtitle, or even a due date for the book because I was still a bit reluctant and fearful of such an accomplishment.

A few days went by of praying, thinking, and reading *The Circle Maker*, and upon finishing it; I ended up on cloud nine! I was in prayer, and I had invited my friend Bob to prayer that morning. When he arrived, I said, "Hey, I've been having these prayer encounters, and my prayer time has been fueled by this book called *The Circle Maker*." I told Bob that God was going to speak to us in prayer and to be ready! You wouldn't believe what happened next! Bob and I began to pace back and forth in prayer. As I paced, God placed one word on my heart: *outrageous*.

I almost dismissed the word! I started repeating the word in my mind. The more I repeated the word, the more real it became. *Outrageous! Outrageous! Outrageous!* I went from saying the word in my mind to blasting it out of my mouth! Then I began saying, "We are called to be outrageous!" I'm quite the wordsmith, so I ran to my MacBook and Googled the word *outrageous*. It said: *exceeding the limits of what is usual*. When I read that definition, it triggered something in me.

Have you ever had a eureka moment? You might be saying, "What the heck is a eureka moment?" It is what happens when you stumble upon a discovery that results in triumph. In other words, that eureka moment ends up becoming your launching pad for progress! In that moment, when God dropped the word *outrageous* in my heart, I knew it was time to write this book. I am so glad you are reading it; this is your eureka moment—the moment that God is going to use in your life to move you forward.

Did you know that you were designed to move forward? Did you know that if you're not moving you're dead? The good news about God is that He shuns dead things. In fact, the Bible says in Romans 4:17 that God, "…gives life to the dead and calls into being things that were not." In other words, He takes dead things, gives them life, and sets them in motion to fulfill a purpose! Outrageous people are people whom God has set in motion to fulfill a specific assignment that warrants "exceeding the limits of usual." I'm tired of the same old same old cycle of living. You're born, you grow old, and then you die. Isn't life more than living and then dying? I think God would agree that we were created to exceed the limits of usual! Has usual become your normal? Deep down inside of you is a person who desires to exceed the limits of usual. I don't know what your usual is; maybe it's going to college, graduating, getting a good-paying job, a mortgage payment, and 2.5 children. Maybe your usual is: "I'll die a nobody in prison." I want to provoke you to reject usual, and the best way to do that is to exceed usual!

Another word for *usual* is *ordinary*. Have you ever watched the television show "No Ordinary Family"? The show is basically about a family that ends up discovering they had super human powers. The father discovers he has extraordinary strength, the mother discovers that she can run faster than a speeding bullet, the daughter discovers that she can read minds, and the son discovers that he's a twenty-first century Einstein.

I love that TV series. Whenever I watch shows like that, it awakens the sleeping giant. I'm not talking about just any sleeping giant; I'm talking about an outrageous giant with the potential to impact generations for Christ.

"No Ordinary Family" is a simple reminder to me that there is more to you and me than meets the eye; there is actually something deeper going on in all of us. The Bible says that God has placed eternity in our hearts. Eternity! Eternity means that there is no beginning and no end; it is kind of like forever. It's hard for me to wrap my mind around the fact that God has placed in us a sense of "there is something more."

Often times what God has placed in us never gets outside of us because we don't take the time to unearth the outrageous potential that lies within. When I was just a little boy, there was something about me that I could never forget. I was an adventuresome child. There were days that I couldn't wait to get up and go outside. I couldn't wait to grab my little brother and my white bucket. We were on a mission to discover where the gardener snakes were. We'd spend all day turning over boards and digging up dirt just to find one gardener snake. We would seriously put all of our energy into discovering where the gardener snakes were. Guess what? We found gardener snakes. Why? We were looking!

What are you willing to discover? Once we discover how wonderfully made we are by God, the better off we'll be. In the pages ahead, my desire is to paint a clear picture of what it means to be outrageous. It takes guts to exceed the limits of usual. In fact, it takes God to exceed the limits of what is usual. May we be found saying like Paul the Apostle, "I can do all things through Christ who strengthens me" (Phil. 4:13, NKJV). By the time you're done reading this book, my prayer is that you will have recognized that you were made for the outrageous life! You've been apprehended by God to exceed the limits of what is usual! You've been drafted by God to forsake the usual and ordinary for a life without limits. After all, it was Jesus who said, "With God nothing is impossible" (Luke 1:37)!

1 FULL CIRCLE

God has a way of bringing things full circle. I am completely assured that nothing happens by just happening. God cares about every aspect of our lives. In fact, at times it may appear that what you go through is just another episode in life that ends up bringing more detriment than triumph. On the other hand, God thinks differently! The scripture says in Isaiah 55:8-11:

For my thoughts are not your thoughts, neither are your ways my ways," declares the Lord. "As the heavens are higher than the earth, so are my ways higher than your ways and my thoughts than your thoughts. As the rain and the snow come down from heaven, and do not return to it without watering the earth and making it bud and flourish, so that it yields seed for the sower and bread for the eater, so is my word that goes out from my mouth: It will not return to me empty, but will accomplish what I desire and achieve the purpose for which I sent it.

As I look back over my life, I know that God knew exactly what He was doing. In fact, the chaos that I experienced in my past somehow blinded me and tricked me into thinking that I was without hope. I love the genius of God; nothing takes Him by surprise. Before time ever existed, God knew exactly where you would be; He knew exactly what you would go through.

In His foreknowledge, He always makes provisions for you and I to overcome. How do I know? God did just that for me.

I haven't always been where I am today. I love the story of Shadrach, Meshach, and Abednego. If you don't know the story, it's an amazing one. They were a bunch of Jewish 20-somethings who were taken captive by a foreign king and forced to submit to a new government. In the process of residing in a new city, a new life, and a new territory, it ultimately conflicted with their core convictions. The king ended up establishing a decree that affected them. The decree stated that they were to literally bow down and worship this king. The three Hebrew radicals decided that they would not obey the decree, but rather honor the God they served faithfully.

News had reached the throne about the civil disobedience of Shadrach, Meshach, and Abednego. As a result, they were sentenced to the fire. The king ordered that they be tied up and dropped into the fire and left for dead.

I don't know about you, but I would have started sweating bullets if I knew that I was about to die. But not these three! They willingly were dropped into the fire. The king thought he had accomplished a great victory. Nonetheless, something happened to these three radical world changers; they were dropped into the fire, but not destroyed.

This supernatural phenomenon caught the attention of the king. In fact, he looked inside of the huge fiery furnace and saw not just the three who were thrown in, but also another. That other person was none other than the pre-incarnate Christ making sure that nothing happened to the three Hebrew boys.

The king instantaneously ordered their release. God had brought about a great victory that day. They came out of the fire and not a hair on their bodies had been singed. God knows how to bring you out of overwhelming difficulties unharmed!

If we're not careful, we can look at people's lives that have made it and think, *oh, they just arrived where they are, and they've made it; it's all good in their life.* For the three Hebrew boys, it didn't start off all good. They were taken from their native land, held captive, and forced to be a part of a kingdom that was contrary to their value system as sons of God.

By all accounts, we could look at their lives after they came out of the fire and assume they have an "all-good" life.

Even though I've come out of the fire, I have a story to tell. The three Hebrew boys have a story to tell. Did you know that there is always a story behind the story? What happened to those three Hebrew boys was indeed outrageous; it exceeded the limits of usual. Things like that don't usually happen. People don't usually survive fiery furnaces. Moreover, people don't just come out of hell like that without there being someone behind the scenes working for their good. There was someone behind the scenes working in my life, even when I was in the fire.

The reason I relate to that story so much is because of the fiery furnaces I've come out of. If it had not been for Jesus Christ being present in my fires, I will admit that I would have died a long time ago.

I come from a family steeped in drugs, immorality, brokenness, crime, and dysfunction. I come from a family of abuse, failed relationships, and chaos. For years my mother struggled to make it as a single parent in the ghetto. For me, the toughest part about being raised in a single-parent home was living with seeing the emotional and psychological pains of my mother. She tried her best to cover up and mask the trauma of having to raise five kids. It didn't help that I added to the pain. I was a kid full of bitterness and rage. That bitterness and rage was expressed in my disobedience and in my excessive lack of respect for my mother. On several occasions I recall secretly wishing that my mom would just die.

Part of my desire to see her defaced from this earth was the emotional trauma that went on in my home. On several occasions my siblings and I experienced emotional abuse that scarred me for many years. One thing that bothered me extremely was how my mother would cuss and yell at us. When we weren't obeying her, whippings and yelling would follow. My mom would call my sister words like "heifer." I didn't know what a heifer was back then, but I knew it wasn't good. Imagine getting yelled at and whipped when you did something wrong! The yelling eventually shut me up emotionally. The more my mom yelled at me for things I did wrong, the more I shut down. And the more I shut down, the more bondage I was in. This shutting down taught me to never share my feelings and to always hold on to what was going on inside of me. The more those feelings of hurt, anger, and bitterness emerged, the more I stuffed them deep down inside of me to the point where I became an emotional wreck. My emotional wreckage manifested in constantly fighting in school.

As I reflect on those early years, I now see why I got into so many fights. I felt helpless against my mother. I felt like I had no voice. I felt like I had no one to stand up for me when she would stand over me and use obscene language that cut me wide open and left me bleeding emotionally.

Stability was not a reality in my home. Just when I thought we were settling down in an apartment, project, or house, we were moving again. That ultimately developed in me a sense of uncertainty of where we were going to live. In fact, growing up, shelters were a reality in my life. I don't know about you, but that does something to a kid when he or she doesn't have a place to call home. Have you ever lived in a homeless shelter?

Ultimately, that transient lifestyle built within me bitterness toward my mother. Honestly, at times I hated my mother. I hated her for how our lives were. I hated her for abandoning us to drugs, jail, and frivolous immoral acts. You'll find that in a community like that, one thing is consistent across the board: anger. The community I live in, North Omaha, is full of angry kids who have been hurt by their parents.

At the root of our anger in this community is hurt. We've been hurt by our parents and the ones who said they loved us but then betrayed us in ways that have scarred many of us for life.

The greatest thing that I missed, needed, and always longed for was a father. I can remember playing basketball for the Omaha Housing Authority. We had games on the weekends and sometimes weeknights. For some reason I always looked in the stands to see if my father would ever show up. Granted, my father never played a significant role in my life, but I always had this hopeful confidence that just maybe one day he would come marching into the basketball game with the greatest cheer a son could ever ask for. It never happened.

There was a kid on our basketball team named Bacarri. He was an amazing basketball player. I'm not sure where he is today, but I'm sure he went on to play basketball at some D-1 school in America. How do I know that? Bacarri not only had an amazing shot and great ball-handling skills, but he also had a dad.

Deep down inside I envied Bacarri. His dad showed up for every game and all of the practices. His dad believed in him. I could see Bacarri's confidence; it was a confidence I lacked. While his dad was affirming his greatness, my dad was deactivating mine. I lived with this lack of confidence for years. As a result, I affirmed my own greatness in not-so-great ways.

At the age of 12, I started experimenting with cigarettes and sex. I think back to those days and often weep at how my virginity at that age was snatched from me by another young lady who was also looking for validation and security. We were two experimenting, validation-seeking adolescents who misunderstood what life was all about. As a result, we both did each other a great disservice. The sad reality encompassing all of my brokenness was that I was masking it well.

One way in which I masked the brokenness was by taking advantage of opportunities to be in the spotlight. I sought to please people left and right. I remember being willing to do anything to get people to like me. I'd do idiotic, adolescent things like break into houses and steal things that didn't belong to me. This gave me a sense of significance. It felt like I mattered. Deep down I think I wanted to know that I mattered, and when I felt like I didn't, I was willing to do whatever it took to attain it.

By the age of 14, I was hanging out with gangbangers. The more I surrounded myself with these guys, the more I became one of them. I desperately wanted to fit in. Every young kid's dream in the ghetto is to be the richest, hardest, and most powerful person on the block. Honestly, the gang lifestyle attracted me. When I looked at the older gang members, they carried themselves in a way that seemed as if they were on top of the world. Because I'd been at the bottom all of my life, I saw the lifestyle of a gang member as a rite of passage into notoriety. I wanted to be the person everyone looked up to. I wanted to be the person people looked to for direction. I wanted to become the very thing I was missing in life. I was lacking a healthy father figure, and I was lacking moral direction. The gang lifestyle offered me just that: leaders, power, money, and drugs. With all of those "perks" came great disappointment and hurt.

In that season of my life, friends were dying from gun violence. The saddest thing happened around that time: I had a cousin who was a great kid, but I started noticing him hanging out more and more in the neighborhood. He went from his birth name to a hood name. When he got his hood name—or his gang name—he starting behaving according to his name. As a result, he ended up losing his life. He died in the same neighborhood that he stood for. Such is the reality for so many across this country; they're falling to their death because they're standing for a gang.

I was a very promiscuous guy. I didn't know what it meant to be faithful to a girl, mainly because I had no clue what faithful was or what it looked like. I had no model for faithfulness! As a result, I ended up getting a girl pregnant. I was only 15 years old at the time, not to mention I'd dropped out of high school around the same time. I never grew up in church. But, there were times and instances in my life in which God was trying to get my attention.

When I was a kid and we lived in the projects, there was an older white guy named Mr. Charlie whom I really liked. He made me feel special; he genuinely cared for me. Every so often Mr. Charlie would pull up in his old school van, jump out of the driver's side, stretch his arms out really wide, and I'd go running into his arms as if I hadn't seen him for years. Those were the days. Although I couldn't articulate it then, there was surely something different about him, not to mention the dentures he had and how he would every now and then pop them out at me. I would get in the van, and Mr. Charlie would take me to some kind of children's center. I can't remember if it was a church or not, but I do remember feeling an overwhelming sense of joy and security when I went. I'm pretty sure they taught me some scriptures and told me that Jesus loved me, but honestly I can't remember any of that. The only thing I can remember is Mr. Charlie and how I knew beyond a shadow of a doubt that he loved me. I'm sure Mr. Charlie has gone on to be with Jesus, as that was 20 years ago, but that is one small yet huge way God used an old white guy to sow spiritual seeds into my life that would one day yield a harvest.

Any time God is trying to get your attention, He will do whatever it takes to get it. There were times when I "was not far from the kingdom of God." There were times I'd go to church for a couple of weeks and then jump right back in the flow of drugs, gangs, and ultimately, crime.

One day, after moving from North Omaha to South Omaha, I was at the table having lunch with my mother, sister, and aunt. For some reason my mother got up from the table, maybe to use the restroom. After a few moments of being gone, she rushed back into the room and looked at my aunt and said, "God said, 'Cast that demon out of Myron!'" This was around the time my mother was trying to get her life back together and had attended church services for a few months, and occasionally, attended with her. When I heard her say those words, instantly a demon took possession over me, made me stand up, and from there began flipping over chairs and making an obscene sound that you only see and hear on horror movies. My aunt calmly got up, looked me in the eye and said, "In the name of Jesus, I command you to stop."

My aunt was a Christian, but I didn't even know she was and that she went to church. When she commanded the demon in me to stop, the demon literally stopped and stood their growling at her for about a span of ten seconds. After that, the demon began to shriek and throw me around a bit. That's when my aunt looked at me and said, "What is your name?" The demon yelled back, "Rebellion!" My aunt yelled in a loud voice, "In the name of Jesus, come out of him!" I instantly felt this demonic force jump out of my body, and I fell to the ground. That type of experience will scare you straight!

I was in church the week after that experience! I actually started reading the Bible and asking questions, and God brought an amazing pastor into my life who really cared for me when I was going through difficult times. As I look back, I see how God used that incident to get my attention. But, a couple months later, I was back in the streets.

Around the age of 16, I got into crime heavily. I tried selling drugs when I was a teenager. I started off purchasing weed from the weed man but quickly discovered that selling weed wouldn't work because I kept getting high off of my own supply.

From there I started selling crack cocaine on the streets of North Omaha. I was a small time drug pusher out to make money so that I could become the next ghetto superstar. It never happened. I was horrible at selling drugs because I'd make my money back and then go buy liquor and weed. It didn't help that I loved to be the center of attention and loved a good party. So, by the end of the night, I'd end up broke.

The second reason I failed to be the best drug pusher was because of how it affected my mother. It weakened me to see that the same drugs I was giving another man's mom were the drugs other guys were selling to my mom. I remember going home one day and seeing my mother with her hair everywhere, her eyes red, and her face completely oblivious to reality. I always knew when my mother was using because she would get extremely generous. She would try to offer me fast food and let me roam around the projects. Deep down I knew what was going on; she was trying to get rid of me because she knew that I knew she was using again. I felt hopeless. I wanted to help my mom, but I was powerless. I ran out of the house in tears and slamming the screen door behind me. I didn't know what to do! The battle of drugs in my mom's life has always been a monster in her closet. It destroyed me to see my mom on the losing end of crack cocaine. I think the affect drugs had on my mind was the biggest deterrent that led me to give up selling drugs. The second largest deterrent was me finding another way to make money that was fast, efficient, and lucrative: robbery. At the age of 15, I committed my first robbery. I started hanging around another crowd of older guys. I would go over to their house to smoke their weed for free and party all night. I started noticing something. They always had money to buy cigarettes, weed, and beer. I asked them, "Hey, where you getting all this money?" They laughed at me!

We all sat down, and they told me that they were in to robbing stores. I looked at them and told them they were crazy and that they could go away for a long time. The more they talked about how easy it was, the more I became interested in exploring that easy way of making money. They told me that all I had to do was plan the robbery good enough to get away and that they would help me with my first robbery.

One night we got in their car with our guns and headed to a convenience store out west. My heart was pounding. I was considering getting of out the car, but deep down I knew there was no turning back. I was hungry for money.

The closer we got to the store, the more I started to sweat. One of the guys reassured me that it was going to be okay and that we would get a lot of money. The elder of the group took the shotgun and put it in my hand. I was scared! I had never held a shotgun before in my life! It was now time to go in. They gave me specific instructions to follow, and I followed them well. We pulled off on a back street, put our masks on, and with guns in our hands, ran into the store. It felt like a movie. I'd never robbed anyone before. This was different than any other crime I had committed. I cocked the shotgun and demanded the clerk to put the money in the bag. The clerk filled the bag, and within 30 seconds we were in and out. We ran back to the car, hopped in, and rolled out. It was done. We got away.

From then on, I was untouchable. I mean, to put a gun in somebody's face and have him or her do what I wanted them to do did something to my confidence. It made me feel powerful. It made me feel like I was in control. It made me feel like I could do something to change my future—at least financially. Most of all, it made me feel invincible.

I must have gone on a robbery spree for almost a year without getting caught. All of that changed as I walked into a Pizza Hut delivery joint with a facemask and a plastic gun. I put the plastic gun in the clerk's face (hoping she wouldn't see that it was a fake gun) and demanded that she fill the bag. She filled it with thousands of dollars, and as she filled it, I grew in great anticipation of how I was going to use that money to change my future. But it never happened. Two hours later I was caught.

One thing I learned is that you can't keep doing wrong and expect good results. There I sat in the Douglas County Youth Center—where I'd been several times before but not for robbery—booked on charges of robbery and use of a weapon to commit a felony, facing up to 100 years in prison. Eventually, the judge sentenced me to prison for 2 to 3 years—at the age of 16. I had been to the local juvenile detention center several times, but this was different. They sent me to juvenile prison: the Nebraska Correctional Youth Facility.

Prison was a different world. You play by a different set of rules. Prison is a place where you're told when to eat, when you can use the bathroom, and when it's time to go to bed. The reason why I didn't feel too fearful was that I knew that although it was a prison, it was still a prison for youth. On top of that, I was still involved in gangs, so I knew that when I finally got to prison I'd have friends from my gang whom I could clique up with once I got there.

I sat in prison for 14 months, and it was a long 14 months. For some, over time prison does something to your psyche. It's not just the physical absence from society behind locked doors that affects you; it's the mental anguish of knowing you're going to be in for a while. It's the emotional drainage of leaving behind family members and kids. It's the humiliating moniker you get when you enter the prison sentence.

Once you enter prison, everyone is given a number. That number is how prison officials identify you. It's set up in a way that makes you an object instead of a person. Somehow I managed to finagle my way out of prison 14 months later. Through a series of drug classes, mental health classes, and obtaining my GED, the system had confidence that I had changed. They were wrong. After my release, I quickly found two jobs. I worked during the day and smoked weed and hung in the projects at night.

A couple of months after my release, I got my first drug test and failed it! Fortunately, my parole officer was a great guy. They gave me another chance to get it together.

Five months after my release on parole, I was back in jail with similar charges, facing the 100 years plus another 100 years, for a total of 200 years in prison. The irony in of all it was the events that led up to the second arrest.

Three days before I was arrested, I'd done a series of robberies—all of which had failed. The second attempted robbery almost cost a guy his life. I had arranged for one of my younger homies to set up a guy who had been from a different gang and had switched his allegiance to us. I hadn't taken the switch very well, so I had him set up to be robbed by me.

I arranged for us to "accidentally" run into each other since we were both in the same apartment complex that night. We both came out of different apartments "at the same time." I pulled out my gun and told him to give me all of his money. For some reason, he wouldn't. I told him one more time, "Give me the money, or I'm going to kill you!" He would not give me the money. By this time a whole host of people were surrounding me. I had to make a quick choice because my reputation was on the line. If he gave me the money, I would prove to be the craziest of all the gang members, and I would gain credibility. If he didn't give me the money, I could be looked at as store cotton.

I pulled the trigger. As I pulled the trigger, it seemed as if all of time stopped. The gun would not fire. I tried two more times to pull the trigger, but it would not fire. Everyone around me was shocked, and no one dared to say anything. I walked away. As I was walking away, I looked at my gun and saw that it was on safety. God was at work behind the scene because I did not put that gun on safety; I almost never did.

The next night I got arrested for another robbery that had gone bad. I tell people that God caught me 10 years ago so that He could change me. At 1 a.m. on March 21, 2002, I entered a jail cell completely tired and broken. The police had cornered me, taken me back to the crime scene where the victim whom I had attempted to rob and kill identified me, and from there I was booked on several charges ranging from attempted assault to attempted robbery to use of a weapon to commit a felony—on top of my previous charges that I was still on parole for.

As I sat in my jail cell that night, I called my girlfriend and told her that it was over because I was going away for a long time. She sat completely silent on the other end of the line. She was stunned. She didn't know what to say, so she said nothing. Full of anguish and sorrow, after what seemed like a decade of silence, I decided to hang up the phone.

I started to dial the next person on my list. As I dialed the number, I went into depression at a speed of 1 to 100 mph! The phone rang and rang and rang. The more the phone rang, the more the reality of what I had done rang, and that reality of the horrible decision to victimize another soul hit me like a tone of bricks. She finally answered the phone; it was my grandmother.

"Granny, I messed up again!" I was sobbing uncontrollably. "I messed up again; I'm in jail! Granny, I messed up my life!" I was gasping for air at that point. There was nothing anybody could have done, and I knew it. I knew I was at the end of my rope, that I had hit rock bottom. My grandmother knew that I had reached the breaking point. She remained silent, just like my girlfriend. Eventually, I hung up the phone completely in another world of fear, regret, and hopelessness.

With all of the energy I could muster up, I dropped to knees in that dimly lit concrete jail cell and began to weep and sob uncontrollably. All alone in that jail cell with no one to understand the pain of my past and the agony of my present, I prayed, "Jesus, I'm destroying my life, but if you change me, I will serve you." I liken this amazing experience to a passage of scripture that amplifies what actually happened that early morning 10 years ago:

> Two men went up to the Temple to pray, one a Pharisee, the other a taxman. The Pharisee posed and prayed like this: 'Oh, God, I thank you that I am not like other people—robbers, crooks, adulterers, or, heaven forbid, like this taxman. I fast twice a week and tithe on all my income.' Meanwhile the tax man, slumped in the shadows, his face in his hands, not daring to look up, said, 'God, give mercy. Forgive me, a sinner.' Jesus commented, "This tax man, not the other, went home made right with God. If you walk around with your nose in the air, you're going to end up flat on your face, but if you're content to be simply yourself, you will become more than yourself. (Luke 18:10-14, MSG)

God exonerated the tax man in spite of his horrible past, and he walked away with the mercy of God on his life. That night when I prayed, I received the mercy of God. I was forgiven for all of the chaos, crime, mayhem, and sin that had disrespected God. I prayed an outrageous prayer! All of heaven stood to attention as I surrendered my life to Jesus Christ. All of heaven rejoiced that one sinner had received new life! I received an outrageous life-altering experience by Jesus Christ himself.

I'm not saying that all of my problems were fixed or even that my circumstance changed, but one thing is for sure: Jesus Christ gave me a new heart that night! I made up in my mind that Jesus Christ was Lord and Savior of my life and that I was going to do a 180 and trust Him to save me, cleanse me, and make me a new creation. The Bible says:

> If you declare with your mouth, 'Jesus is Lord,' and believe in your heart that God raised him from the dead, you will be saved. For it is with your heart that you believe and are justified, and it is with your mouth that you profess your faith and are saved. (Rom. 10:9-10)

Regardless of where you are in life and what side of the tracks you grew up on, all of us have to come to grips with the fact that Jesus Christ is the deciding factor of whether our not you exceed usual. This world usually lives without Jesus; that doesn't have to be you. You can decide right now that you are going to pray an outrageous prayer. You can decide that you will bow your knee, turn your back on living for yourself, and with conviction and faith declare that Jesus is now Lord and Savior of your life and that because He died on an old, rugged cross for your sin, you can receive mercy and forgiveness of sin and have a fresh start. In spite of where you are right now, an outrageous life is possible. I encourage you to put this book down right now and simply say to Jesus:

> "I turn away from my sin and living for myself. Jesus, You are now the Lord and Savior of my life. I trust that you died for my sins so that I might be forgiven. Cleanse me. Fill me with your presence and use me to be a radical world changer so that I can make an outrageous difference in our world."

Friend, if you declared and prayed that from your heart, the Bible makes it clear that you are now a forgiven and free child of God with a fresh start. It's not going to be peaches and cream every day, but you can always go to the One who owns the peaches and cream; His name is Jesus. Please get in touch with me, find me on Facebook, or email me. I promise I will email you back. I'd love to hear your *outrageous* story!

Myron Pierce

2 BEFORE & AFTER PICTURES

Have you ever watched an infomercial that promised fat loss results? The whole infomercial is designed to inform you that what they have to offer is completely essential to a life-transforming experience. Whatever the program or pill is, the promise is: *if you try us, we won't disappoint you.* In fact, they do two things to draw you in: they show you a picture, and they tell you the stories. The marketing ploy is designed to get you to see what you can become because they know if they can get your attention by casting vision and telling a story, they have a great chance at getting your money. As I sat awaiting sentencing in 2002, God put a desire in my heart to become a before-and-after picture for those connected to me, which included my family, friends, and close associates. If you were to take a snap shot of my past, you would definitely see a young kid trapped in bondage, full of anger, hurt, and rage. You would see a kid with a dysfunctional family who lacked holistic parenting. You would see a kid without a dad;

you would see a bastard. You would see a kid experimenting with sex, drugs, crime, and violence. You would see a kid who eventually became a teenager and struggled with identity issues, insecurities, and addictions. You would see a teenager looking for love in all the wrong places. You would see a teenager searching for freedom in high-bondage areas. You would surely see a broken and disheartened soul wanting out—out of the drugs, crime, and depression. God saw my past. But, the same God who sees our past and present is the same God who sees our future.

The Lord eventually brought further clarity to the desire of being a before-and-after picture. He was calling me to be used by Him to simply be a picture of faith, hope, and love. I sensed that He wanted me to step out of the boat and walk on the waters of impossibilities so that others could see that only He is God and that Jesus Christ alone saves.

Did you know that God is in the business of giving us His desires so that they can be displayed in our lives? God did just that with the desire He gave me to truly be a before-and-after picture for people, that they might consider the product and that Jesus actually does love them, want them, and desire an amazing relationship with them.

I had a friend who is now deceased. I used to look up to him because of the status he had in the gang life. His nickname was *Twig*. Everybody loved him. He was the kind of guy that you just wanted to hang around. Twig had so much potential. He was the go-to man full of passion, vigor, and leadership. Those very values in the hand of someone not serving Jesus ends in disaster.

I got an opportunity to see Twig before he died. Twig got booked on several felony charges the same year I was awaiting sentencing. He actually was assigned to the same cellblock as I. I still remember the day he walked into the cellblock. We instantly shook hands, hugged, and sat down to talk. He didn't know that I'd become a Christian because he was out running the streets. As we sat and talked, he started to notice something different about me. I wasn't cursing, I wasn't using obscene language, and I wasn't talking about our gang. I could tell by the look on his face that inside he was wrestling with what was different about me. At that point I felt it was time to tell Twig what had happened.

With my palms sweating and my heart pounding, I blurted out, "I'm a Christian now." I'll be honest, before I said that statement, fear was literally choking me. I was fearful that I wouldn't be accepted, fearful that I'd get ridiculed, and fearful that he'd tell everyone and that I'd be treated as an outcast. But something different happened. I can't remember the entire conversation, but what I do remember is him smiling and the spark of interest that he had. God was answering the desires of my heart—*that I'd be a before-and-after picture of God's grace and love.*

As months progressed, Twig asked more question like, "What happened?" "How did you become a Christ follower?" "Why do you believe that?" One of the most profound questions Twig asked me was, "Can you order me the same Bible studies you're doing?" The before-and-after picture was sending a powerful message: *you can be changed!*

I sat down with Twig and personally filled out the information card, mailed it off, and within a few weeks Twig was doing Bible studies through correspondence! Every day I would make sure Twig was doing his studies. He'd have questions about Jesus, and we'd simply sit down and have long conversations about what it meant to serve God. I knew deep down that Twig wanted to serve Jesus; I knew the before-and-after picture was compelling.

Eventually, Twig got released from jail. I was sad that he was leaving, but glad that God had given him an opportunity to respond to Jesus. I don't know whether or not Twig ever did receive Jesus. We had multiple conversations about Him and the sacrifice He made on our behalf so that we could experience the forgiveness of God and a fruitful life, but he never said yes.

The same week Twig got out of jail is the same week he made a foolish decision. He killed a cop, and as a result, he lost his life as well. The day I received the news, I was devastated. Here one day and gone the next. I didn't know what to think. I sat and wept, deeply grieved at how two lives were lost because of one decision. I often ask, *what if Twig would have made a decision to serve Christ?* In retrospect, God was using me. God had arranged for an infomercial to be presented to Twig, and He showed him a before-and-after picture of a life-changing, sin-losing product called Jesus. Where are you at right now? You've begun reading this outrageous before-and-after picture of my life, but right here in the fourth chapter, I sense God saying, *what will you do with the before-and-after picture?* Friends, we have a choice to reach out and embrace the truth about what God can do in our lives. Maybe take some time to reflect and ask as many questions as you want. I know you have questions, and God is in the business with providing you enough insight to make a decision about your transformation. God wants you to lose what's holding you down. He wants to see a full body makeover done in your life, but it's all on your. What will you do with this Outrageous Infomercial? For some of you, you know that God is calling you to become an Outrageous Infomercial for your family and friends, but you've been playing it safe. You've been saying *I'll get it together one day, I'll get serious eventually.* My friend, that's a dangerous line to walk. There's more to life than what you want. What about what He wants. What if your life actually matters? What if your before and after picture real can make a difference in the grand scheme of things. You have an Outrageous opportunity to become the change God wants to see.

I'm humbled that God would allow me to serve Twig those few months in jail together. Even if all my questions aren't answered about why, I know at the end of the day God was chasing after Twig. At the end of the day God was trying to engage Twig in such a way that he'd buy in to the product, and for that I'm grateful that the desire I becoming a before and after picture is still occurring in my life. Countless lives have seen and heard the outrageous nature of Jesus and his ability to take a life, snatch me from the clutch of death itself, and put me in a spacious place to change the world.

3 DREAM SHEETS & IMPOSSIBILITIES

The biggest blessing in my life was having the time to get to know God as I awaited sentencing. I knew I was guilty of breaking the law, and it made no sense to me to play around with my fate. God apprehended me the night I got arrested, and I knew that I had to face the consequences for my wrongdoing.

The reality was that I'd been guilty of criminal activity, and I'd later be sentenced. The other side of the coin was that I'd been declared "not guilty" before the court of heaven; in God's eyes I was completely forgiven of all my sin.

I lived with those two worlds for eight months as I awaited sentencing, and those days were glorious. I saw so many people impacted for Jesus while I was in county jail. I remember the first cellblock that I went to called Mod 3, which was where all of the young guys were. In reality, I had surrendered my life to Jesus and became a missionary to the cellblock. No one had to ask me to read my Bible; I devoured it. I started teaching Bible studies within the first week of my incarceration, and there were around ten guys who attended. In a very real way, that was my first church plant! We would all open the Bible together and go around the circle taking turns reading the Scripture. From there I would break down the scriptures and provide insight into what the Word of God was saying. With no theological education, I led my first Bible study! It was a hit! Bible study grew into cellblock prayer, which happened every night. We gathered together and held hands before the lights went out. Before opening prayer, guys would recite a scripture that was near and dear to their hearts, while others even recited poems.

In the midst of waiting for sentencing, God continued to knit my heart to Him. He began to show me that I had to completely sever my old identity from my new identity, and He did that by using a rival gang member. The first day I entered Douglas County Correctional Center, I was confronted with this man. As soon as I stepped into Mod 3, he approached me and said, "What hood you from?" I looked him in his eyes, stuck out my frail chest, and told him. Ironically enough, he turned and walked away. There was still gang paraphernalia from my past that God wanted to completely purge me from, and He did that primarily by giving me more of a desire to serve, read the Bible and faith-provoking Christian books, and sharing my faith with others in Mod 3. The longer I sat, the more I saw how God was molding me and preparing me for something great.

It wasn't long before I started Bible studies through correspondence. I was so hungry to learn the word of God and tell others about Jesus! The more I read and studied, the more I shared what I was learning. As I saturated myself with truth, God began unraveling snippets of my future.

One day I received a note card in the mail from one of my correspondence teachers. The only thing she'd written on the note card was a scripture, Jeremiah 29:11: "'For I know the plans I have for you,' declares the Lord, 'plans to prosper you and not to harm you, plans to give you hope and a future'" (NIV). The words leapt off that little note card and into my heart! I could not believe what I was reading! It was as if God was saying, "I know you're in a bad spot right now, but I want you to trust that I know what I'm doing in your life and that I really do have a future for you."

Something happened to me that day as I read that scripture. Hope sprang up in my soul; there was more pep in my step and, ultimately, my perspective.

I remember the first time I rode on an airplane; it was so scary! First of all, I have seasonal acrophobia (fear of heights). So, getting on an airplane was a big deal.

The moment we took off, I noticed something almost instantly: it looks a lot different in the air than on the ground. That may not be news for you, but for someone who had never been that high in his life, it was a big deal! As we flew out of Omaha, Nebraska, all of a sudden the houses looked smaller—everything looked smaller. When I read Jeremiah 29:11, God, in a way, buckled me in, and I got into airplane mode! It was as if that scripture was Airline Jeremiah 29:11 and that I'd departed and would shortly be arriving at Freedom Airport. The hard times that I would soon face looked small because my perspective had changed, and the catalyst for such change of perspective was that one scripture.

On October 8, 2002, I entered the courtroom to be sentenced for attempted robbery and use of a weapon to commit a felony. I was ready. I was ready to go on with the next phase of my life. God had prepared my heart for what would happen next.

There in the courtroom was my family, my public defender, the judge, and Jesus. As the judge opened his mouth, it was as if all time stood still. I stood before the judge waiting to hear how much time I was about to receive. The next thing you know, the judgment had been pronounced: 14 to 30 years. Have you ever been at a lost for words? After I'd heard the judgment, I was a bit dumbfounded. I was waiting at any moment to wake up out of that horrific dream. I looked back at my family after the judgment and began to wail. I could not believe that I was going away to prison for that long.

As I walked out of the courtroom in shock, I distinctly remember praying, "God, I'm going to serve you regardless of the sentence. When I get to prison, I will serve you completely." By faith I made that statement, but I was definitely shaken up at the news I had just received. Still, deep down I knew that I knew that God was in control. I almost felt like that was the perfect opportunity to trust God.

Have you ever been in a situation where you were expecting one thing and got another? I was not expecting that much time, and it through me for a loop. One thing is for sure: nothing takes God by surprise. We may be taken aback by situations and circumstances as they arise, but in those times when we don't understand, we have to embrace it, roll with it, and trust that in the end everything will work out. In my shock, I made a decision to trust God. You may be in a shocking scenario right now in this season of your life. God is not intimidated by what shocks you. Stay the course. I learned that day in the courtroom that life is a series of choices. After all, I made a series of choices that landed me in that courtroom. It would later be another series of right choices that would land me right in the middle of God's will.

Shortly after my sentencing, I was shipped off to Lincoln, Nebraska to the Diagnostic and Evaluation Center—the place every prisoner goes before entering prison to be processed and evaluated to see where he or she will eventually be placed.

One thing you learn very quickly when you are incarcerated is the importance of money and mail; they are commodities in prison. You would be amazed at how much a piece of mail would mean to a prisoner. The crazy thing is that when you're incarcerated, you don't care who you get mail from, even if it's from the administration. If it's just a little slip saying, "Go to the nurse," you take it even on your worst day.

One day I received a piece of in-house mail; it was a half sheet of paper, which everyone in prison calls a "dream sheet" although I have no idea why it is called that because of what it is. On it was my information about my sentencing structure. I'd been sentenced to 14 to 30 years in prison. What that ultimately should have meant was that I could possibly get out on parole after seven years, but according to my dream sheet, under "Parole Eligibility" it said, "Not eligible."

I did a double take when I read those words, "Not eligible," which are two words that no incarcerated person ever wants to hear. I'm no rocket scientist, but I knew what that meant: NOT ELIGIBLE! My heart sank, my world came tumbling down, and my hope dwindled. "Not eligible" meant that I would be getting released in 2018, and it was only 2002. I'd be spending close to the next 16 years in prison! I cried. I could not swallow the news. It was so alarming because the judge had told me that I would be eligible for release in seven years. Untrue.

After standing there completely stunned over the news I'd received, something happened to me. I felt this overwhelming confidence. I felt like someone had filled me up with faith and supercharged me with courage.

The next thing you know I was ripping up the dream sheet! I trashed it, ran to my prison cell, slammed the door, and fell on my knees in tears. Then these words came to my mind: "'For I alone know the plans that I have for you,' declares the Lord, plans to prosper you and not to harm you, plans to give you a future and a hope.'"

That day God solidified my future. In a very real way, God reconfirmed the future that He had for me. It was as if all time stopped, and in that holy moment, God wrapped His arms around me and gave me comfort that I can only describe as warm, securing, and confirming.

Deep down I knew that something would change because I knew that with God all things were possible.

4 THE POINT OF NO RETURN

Nothing "just happens." Everything that happens is a result of something that was set in motion. For instance, a car doesn't move without someone shifting gears. Once you shift a car from park to drive, you set the car in motion in a direction that ultimately causes the car to move from point A to point B. The same is true of your life. You are where you are because something shifted. As a result of the shift, you've either moved forward or backward.

In prison, people are constantly shifting. One thing that is for sure in prison is that there are a lot of people going forward, and there are a lot of people going backward. In other words, I heard a lot of negative words that people spoke over their lives based on a variety of things. One constant reoccurring statement was, "This is all I know." From what I've gathered, deep down at the heart of such a statement like that is a sense of hopelessness. And hopelessness will shift you backward. After thinking deeply about hopelessness in prison, I've come to the conclusion that hopeless people will always fall back instead of move forward. At the end of the day, that type of disposition didn't just happen. A series of small steps result in huge results that can either work for you or against you. Part of the reason people never move forward in prison is because they've allowed themselves to be captivated by a lie that triggered a thought that resulted in a way of thinking, which ended up producing a lifestyle of fear.

I empathize with my brothers in prison who have the mindset, *this is all I know*. I understand what it's like to be at the end of your rope. I understand what it feels like to be missing something but to not be sure what exactly it is you're missing. We've all been in a place of being unsure of how to process the brokenness, hurt, and bad decisions that resulted in the plans of God being hindered in our lives. It's tough when you're in prison because you're constantly reminded of where you are. It's as if you never get a break from recognizing where you are, why you are, and how you got there. I actually think it's a part of the whole prison experience. It's designed in such a way that you will never forget what got you there in the first place.

I remember the first day I left the Diagnostic and Evaluation Center (D&E) to head to Lincoln Correctional Center (LCC). The two facilities are actually connected to each other, so for those who get classified and then sent to LCC, the trip from one to the next takes virtually 10 minutes. If you've ever seen "The Green Mile," you will remember when the big, buff Black guy, Michael Clarke Duncan, walked down that long hallway to get executed or sent to his cell. That's what the walk from the D&E is like; it's a long hallway that connects one facility to the other.

The traumatizing trip through that underground tunnel is unforgettable. I call it "the green mile." First off, the guards cuff your hands and your ankles. From there, they take a chain and connect the cuffs to where you're shackled from the wrists to the ankles. They make it impossible to escape. I felt so alone. That long, 10-minute trip was the most reflective time of my life. I couldn't help but think about what had led me to that point. All kinds of thoughts crossed my mind, as I got closer to the place where I would spend a pretty significant amount of time.

There's something about the unfamiliar. With unfamiliarity, for me, came a sense of fear and anxiety, and it was all because I just didn't know what to expect. I had been to the juvenile prison, but I was sure that it was nothing like what I was about to experience. The sad thing about it is that the movie industry does a good job at creating a horrific picture of what prison is like. So, all kinds of questions came to my mind, *What if someone assaults me? What if I don't make it out alive? What if I get into a fight? What if there's a gang riot? How will I respond? What if someone tries to stab me? What if I get raped? What if I get institutionalized and this becomes my way of life forever?* The closer I got to the end of "the green mile," the greater the fear was.

I finally made it to the end. The only thing that stood between "the green mile" and me was a thick, grey, metal door. As the guard pulled out his key and turned the lock on the door, God began to turn my heart and open the door to courage. He began to remind me that He was with me and that regardless of what happened, I would make it. A feeling of assurance gripped my heart. Although I didn't hear His audible voice as I walked over the threshold of that door, one thing I did feel was, *It's going to be okay, and I'm going to make it.* It was with that assurance that I crossed over and entered LCC.

I have a friend who visits Omaha from time to time, especially during the summer. He hasn't been back to Omaha in quite some time, but the last time he came he made a statement that illuminated my world. He said, "Myron, burn the bridges." In other words, *you can't go back.* The context he used was regarding youth ministry, but I took that statement to heart.

I began to ponder the thought of burning the bridges. I had certainly known how to burn bridges in the past, but this was different. He was telling me to burn bridges in doing people wrong, crossing them, and wearing out my welcome. He was saying, "Get to a point where it's impossible to turn back"—to the point of no return.

I think there are times and junctions in our lives in which God says the same thing. Isaiah 43:18-19 in The Message says:

Forget about what's happened; don't keep going over old history. Be alert, be present. I'm about to do something brand-new. It's bursting out! Don't you see it? There it is! I'm making a road through the desert, rivers in the badlands.

Isn't that what Jesus does? He specializes in helping people burn the bridges. He operates under the notion of not going back to where we used to be. Jesus majors in assisting us in seeing that if we're going to be, live, and see the idea of *outrageous*, we must burn the bridges. We must get to the place where we are all out of options and cannot go back. I told someone the other day, "Your past is a poor predictor of your future." What was I saying is that you've got to get to the point of no return because people who get to that point end up exceeding the limits of usual.

Our world normally majors in moving back rather than forward. Not so with you and me. I have a feeling that you're ready to burn the bridges!

The first day I stepped foot into LCC I had burned the bridges. Regardless of my situation, I was ready to walk in transformation. In spite of receiving new information about my sentencing structure, I was a man on a mission. I would not settle for anything less than an outrageous demonstration of God's work in my life!

Any time you get ready to live for God, burn the bridges, and get to the point of no return, you can almost expect to be tested.

There's one thing you should know about prison: your business is public knowledge. Information about who you are, your crime, and your sentencing structure are leaked before you ever hit the prison yard. One way that I know for sure that this happens is through inmates who work in the prison laundry department.

Every inmate gets a set of clothing. With that clothing is an intake paper with all of your information on it. Although the prison guards are the only ones to see it, at times it gets to the inmates. Prison is like a small rural town. Everybody knows everybody's business, and I wasn't exempt from that.

All of my enemies, associates, friends, and peers were there in prison. I can remember one of my older "homies" from my hood coming up to me—he calls himself a "Triple Original Gangsta"—within the first few days of being at LCC. You've got to know something about this guy: he has muscles bigger than my hamstrings, and his chest is broader than the Nile river (it's a bit of hyperbole, but you get what I'm trying to say). This guy is just downright buff. On the other hand, I was at that time about 180 pounds. It was like David and Goliath all over again.

The first thing he said to me was, "What's up, lil homie?" I still don't know who "lil homie" is, but when Triple O.G. is talking, you'd better be "lil homie." Evidently he knew that I was coming. I said, "What's up?" to him. He poked his chest out and gave me a handshake. I'll be honest, this brother is intimidating!

The next thing he said was, "You wanna smoke this weed, lil homie?" The moment of testing had come. I had to decide if I was burning the bridges or not—if I was truly at the point of no return. You never know if you're at that point until an opportunity is presented to reveal what you really believe to be true.

I stood upright, looked Triple O.G. in the face and said, "No, I'm a Christian now." He looked at me with a puzzled look on his face. I seriously thought I was about to die. I could just see the preacher saying, "We are gathered here today in memory of Myron Raymond Pierce." I snapped out of the open vision of Triple O.G. murdering me just in time to hear him say, "Okay, lil homie. If you gone be with that then be with that, and if you gone be with this, be with this." *He gave me a pass!* It was the favor of God. Anyone in his or her right mind would not say no to Triple O.G. I firmly believe that test catapulted me closer to my destiny. I was at the point of no return. That day solidified my future; I was all in like never before.

I didn't grow up singing hymns. In fact, I didn't know what a hymn was until I got to prison. But, there's a hymn called "I Have Decided to Follow Jesus" by Sadhu Sundar Singh that says:

"I have decided to follow Jesus. I have decided to follow Jesus. I have decided to follow Jesus. No turning back, no turning back. Though none go with me, still I will follow. Though none go with me, still I will follow. No turning back, no turning back. The world behind me, the cross before me. The world behind me, the cross before me. The world behind me, the cross before me. No turning back, no turning back."

    There are times in which what we say we believe will be tested. I think those are precious times that God uses to teach us who He is and what we're made of. I learned a valuable lesson that day. I learned that what you believe and what you say comes with a price. Sometimes that price will be a pass and at others times it may even be your life. Regardless of the price, may we be people who say, "I'm at the point of no return." That is *outrageous*. That kind of response exceeds what usually happens when people are presented with that kind of situation.

5 FAITH IT TILL YOU MAKE IT

What role does faith play in your life? God called Abram to do some pretty crazy things! If you don't know the story, it's amazing! Abram was minding his own business, and God completely interrupted his life and told him:

Go from your country, your people and your father's household to the land I will show you. I will make you into a great nation, and I will bless you; I will make your name great, and you will be a blessing. I will bless those who bless you, and whoever curses you I will curse; and all peoples on earth will be blessed through you. (Genesis 12:1-3)

I don't know about you, but that would spook me a little bit! Abram was living his own life, and something extraordinary happened. God spoke to him. And afterward, Abram had two options: obey or disobey. He had the choice to say yes or no, to have faith in God and completely believe that what He said to him would actually happen, or respond by saying, "Thanks but no thanks."

I love Abram's response: "So Abram went, as the Lord had told him." (Genesis 12:4). What would you have done? If we're honest, most of us would have went to a counselor and said, "I'm hearing voices." But not Abram. Abram went and obeyed.

The quickest way to discover the role of faith in God in your life is to look at your obedience. Obedience is the determining factor of what you believe. For Abram, we can clearly see that he had faith in God; he had faith that God knew exactly what was in store for him. Abram didn't have it all figured out, but he didn't need to hire a consultant to tell him whether or not it would be in the best interest of him and his family. No. *Abram went.* Abram obeyed God. Abram had faith.

It's this same Abram that God eventually spoke to again and told him, "Hey, Abram, your name is no longer Abram, but Abraham." Abraham means "father of many nations." In other words, God told him that he was going to have a son. The only problem was that Abraham was pretty old. God was going off on a tangent providing insight into Abraham's life and future. What did Abraham do? Well, I'd like to say that Abraham allowed God to make it all transpire, but in this instance, Abraham tried to force the will of God to happen by sleeping with his wife's servant, thinking that maybe God would give him a son through her. That was not God's will. Eventually, Abraham got it together, placed his faith in God, and God did a miracle in his wife's body.

I love the story of Abraham! When I read and reflect on this historic story, I see similarities in my life. In 2002 as I was waiting to get sentenced, I got a word from God. I previously shared the story about my teacher sending me a scripture that resulted in my thinking being shifted in a way that I completely believed God. As I sat and read that scripture, Jeremiah 29:11—that God had a plan for my life that involved prosperity, hope, and a future—I couldn't help but believe God. How did that affect my life? I obeyed. You might be thinking, *but Myron, how did you obey?* At that point, the only thing I knew to do was tell people.

When I got to LCC I began running my mouth about that one scripture that God had given me—Jeremiah 29:11. I'd go up to my old friends from the street and say, "I'm getting out of here because God has a plan for my life." Guess what? They laugh at me. I remember telling one guy, and he laughed and said, "I want what you smoking." I didn't let that get to me! In fact, it stirred my faith even more that although I was in prison with a 14- to 30-year sentence, it didn't matter what it looked like at that moment. Deep down I knew that God could not lie. I knew His character was enough to change my circumstances. Another reason I was crazy enough to believe that I was getting out of prison a lot sooner and that I could believe God was because I seen how He changed me. He changed my heart, cleaned up my language, gave me a different outlook on life, and eliminated hopelessness in my soul. If He did that, wouldn't He come through on this other promise? I just knew He would!

After months of running my mouth and telling people that I was getting out before my projected release date, which was October 2018, I stumbled upon another verse:

"Have faith in God," Jesus answered. "Truly I tell you, if anyone says to this mountain, 'Go, throw yourself into the sea,' and does not doubt in their heart but believes that what they say will happen, it will be done for them. Therefore I tell you, whatever you ask for in prayer, believe that you have received it, and it will be yours." (Mark 11:22-24)

Reading about the life of Abraham was one thing, but when I read this scripture it revolutionized my life. The context of it is amazing. Jesus was hungry, He saw a fig tree, went up to it, and found nothing on it. He looked at it and said, "May no one ever eat fruit from you again." Jesus spoke to a fig tree. Who does that? Who speaks to inanimate objects? Jesus! This was my conclusion after reading that scripture: either Jesus was crazy and needed medicine, or He was making a demonstrative statement about the power of faith. His followers were blown away and so was I! I had one conclusion: "It's time to talk to the locks of the prison." I got up every day in that first year and started talking to locks. I made one statement, "You've got to let me go." As time progressed, I made other statements like, "Let me free." At times I went overboard and started speaking to my pillow, "You've been good to me, but I've got to go." People thought I'd lost my mind, but once I got insight into how faith works, I continued speaking to anything I could because I was getting out of prison before 2018! What was I training my heart and mind to do? I was rewiring my way of thinking to line up with how God wanted me to live. I tell people now, "You've got to faith it till you make it."

Faith is no respecter of persons. Jesus said it the best: "Have faith in God" (Mark 11:22). Faith in God will make you strong; it will elevate your thinking and cause you to soar above your present situation. I never denied the facts. Indeed, I was arrested, found guilty, sentenced, and sent to prison with a 14 to 30 year sentence with no opportunity for parole. Indeed, my tentative release date was 2018. But I didn't waver at the promise of God—that He had a three-fold plan for my life that involved prosperity, hope, and a future. I love what the Bible says about Abraham in Romans 4:

Against all hope, Abraham in hope believed and so became the father of many nations, just as it had been said to him, so shall your offspring be. Without weakening in his faith, he faced the fact that his body was as good as dead – since he was about a hundred years old – and that Sarah's womb was also dead. Yet he did not waver through unbelief regarding the promises of God, but was strengthened in his faith and gave glory to God, being fully persuaded that God had power to do what he had promised. When I read that about Abraham that first year, I took those promises and began to live by them in my life. I made a decision that I would:

In hope believe
Not weaken in my faith
Not deny the facts
Not waver through unbelief regarding my promise (Jeremiah 29:11)
Be strengthened in my faith in God
Give God glory
Be fully persuaded that God could deliver on His promise.
Those seven points became the parameters in my life. I refused to go beyond them. In order to not jump over that seven-sided fence, I made

little note cards of different scriptures that reminded me of God's plan for my life. I posted them on my bunk, the toilet, my desk, and in my pocket. One day during that first year in prison, I was in my cell relaxing when my door popped. The caseworker had unlocked my door and was calling me to the office. I went out of my cell and walked to the office. She handed me a letter that was from the State of Nebraska. I quickly went back to my room and opened it. It was a letter saying that I was not eligible for parole. Previously I wasn't eligible because I'd committed prior felonies, and with committing the current felonies, that made me ineligible for an early release. But the law changed seven months later! All I could do was fall on my knees and begin to cry. To see that Jeremiah 29:11 was working on my behalf gave me great courage and resolve! That news confirmed God's call on my life! I felt unstoppable by an irresistible, loving God!

I darted out of my room to share the news with anyone who would listen! "See, I told you! I told you!" For seven months I prayed, read my Bible, told people I was getting out, and spoke to the locks! You have to faith it till you make it!

God is real. His Word is true. Faith in God will transform you, your life, and your world! Faith it till you make it. What has God told you? How have you responded? What will you do? For me, it was clear that God wanted me to get out of prison for reasons that I am still seeing unfold and unravel in my life.

For the past two months, several of us have been getting up at 4:00 a.m. and making it to the church at 4:30 a.m. every day, seven days a week, to simply pray for two and a half hours because we are so hungry for God. Guess what? High schoolers are showing up to pray and seek the face of God! Today, a young lady showed up. She is an amazing young lady, but she came in broken, battered, and bruised. She even came in saying that she was gay and had a girlfriend, but she showed up for prayer after being invited by her sister, who was invited by her brother. All we did was love on her, pray for her, hug her, and tell her that Jesus loves her. For two hours she wept and stretched her hands out to heaven calling out to her Savior. From her own lips she said, "Jesus, I belong to you." It's times like these that I see how the plans of God are being unfolded in my life. Imagine if I was still in prison; I would have never met this young lady who came to see for herself what God was saying to her. After prayer she said, "Now I see what God is doing here, and I want to come back." What if I had never decided to faith it till I made it? What if I would have responded like many of my peers, "This is all I know"? I would still be in prison.

Regardless of where you are in life, God is trying to get your attention. He wants to speak to you. Are you listening? What is He telling you to do? What promise is He making you? I can't answer that for you, but I can promise you that He has something to say, and what He has to say can change your life. When He speaks to you—and He will—do whatever He tells you; your life depends on it. However long it takes to see His promises played out in your life, have the audacity to faith it till you make it because the promises of God are true, real, and relevant to your life. Faith it till you make it!

6 BUILDING WHEN EVERYONE IS LAUGHING

Have you ever been looked at as weird? Have you ever done something that seemed so ridiculous, but you knew that you knew that God told you to do it? Noah in the Bible is a prime example of a person who chose to obey God even when it seemed weird. Hebrews 11 gives a summary of his life:

By faith Noah, when warned about things not yet seen, in holy fear built
 An ark to save his family… (Hebrews 11:7)
You may be thinking, *so what? He built an ark!* I'd agree with you if that were all there was to the story, but it wasn't. What made this situation pretty weird was that in Noah's day it hadn't rained yet. His generation had never seen rain; it didn't exist at the time! The Bible says in Genesis 2:5,

Now no shrub had yet appeared on the earth and no plant had yet sprung up, for the Lord had not sent rain on the earth and there was no one to work the ground, but streams came up from the earth and watered the whole surface of the ground. There you have it! No rain. But Noah was called by God to build the Titanic.
The other problem with building this massive boat was the peer pressure that Noah was sure to receive as a result of building the boat. However, that mattered none to Noah. God wanted him to build the boat to save his family. The whole world had grown wicked and judgment was sure to

come, but because Noah found favor with God and was seen as righteous in His sight, Noah got inside information. Thus, he began to build, and the more he built the more he became the laughing stock of the city. Can you imagine the humiliation and scorn that he experienced all because "God told him to build"?

The story of Noah resonates with me on several levels. In prison, I began to build. No, it wasn't a boat; it was a life. I began to do things to prepare myself for where I knew God wanted to take me. One area in which God began to deal with me was my time, and more importantly, the management of my time. He gave me insight into a little golden nugget. One day it dawned on me that I can manage my time even though the prison system controls it. In other words, God began to speak to my heart, and He impressed upon me to get a calendar and lay out what I would be doing from Monday to Monday.

I would wake up every day at 5:00 a.m. and start my day by watching Christian preachers. From 5:00 a.m. to 7:00 a.m. I'd watch each broadcast and take as many notes as I could on biblical teaching. What was I doing? I was building. I was building into my spiritual life. I was an open container hungry for the words of life. Every morning as I listened to the Bible being taught, a greater desire was created in me to apply what I was being taught. On top of that, it created an even stronger desire to want to communicate God's word!

After getting my daily intake of God's word via Christian television, I'd turn off the TV and spend another hour in His word, reading and studying, studying and reading. Along with that, I'd spend another hour praying. Every day from 5:00 a.m. to 8:00 a.m. I could count on waking up, seeking the face of God, and learning more and more about His ways. I was building.

In prison everyone has to work a job. The first job I landed was working in the prison's kitchen—washing dishes! It was a mundane job, but God taught me something. I learned to turn a horrible work position into an exciting time of worship. As I'd push those dishes through the dishwasher, I'd sing, "It's a new season; it's a new day. A fresh anointing is coming my way. It's a season of power and prosperity. It's a new season, and it's coming to me." What was I doing? I was building. I was learning to worship God even in situations that weren't ideal. And it created in me a sense of thankfulness. Others around me couldn't understand. I was practically known as the singing preacher. I still think I can't sing a lick. I learned valuable lessons about work that I couldn't get anywhere else but a prison. The degrading thing about working in prison is you start out getting paid $1.21 a day. Yes, $1.21 dollars a day! When I got to prison and learned that is how everyone starts out, I was fuming. God was trying to teach me something: to be thankful in all situations. I have to be completely honest; there were days when I didn't feel like getting up. Heck, I didn't even feel like being a Christian, But in those times when I went in with an attitude, I learned that people were watching me. Not only were people watching me but God was also watching me. There's nothing like being reminded by God that I'm called to do whatever I do to the glory of God. I definitely didn't arrive over night, but starting at the bottom of the totem pole with degrading pay, I learned to learn that the type of job and the wage given doesn't define who I am; God does. My attitude shifted, and I started to see that God was building me up to become a mighty man of God.

There are many things that I can share regarding ways in which I built, but this last point is pretty powerful, and I think it's going to change the way you think about this issue. It's about giving. I was sentenced to 14 to 30 years in prison for attempted robbery and use of a weapon to commit a felony. The day I got sentenced I made God a promise. I told him, "When I get to where I'm going, I will be a giver." In the Book of Malachi, it says:

"Will a mere mortal rob God? Yet you rob me. But you ask, 'How are we robbing you?' In tithes and offerings. You are under a curse—your whole nation—because you are robbing me. Bring the whole tithe into the storehouse, that there may be food in my house. Test me in this," says the Lord Almighty, "and see if I will not throw open the floodgates of heaven and pour out so much blessing that there will not be room enough to store it." (Malachi 3:8-10)

In context, God used the prophet Malachi to speak a word to the nation of Israel. God reminded them of their waywardness and confronted them in such a way that they came face to face with how greedy they had become.

The people of God were withholding in the area of finances, which ultimately ended up being a heart issue with them.

The principle for me that I took from these passages was that I didn't want to be guilty being a taker. I had already been sentenced to a significant amount of time because I tried to take by force money that didn't belong to me. I didn't want to be guilty of withholding from God. When I got to LCC, I made sure that every time I got my $36.30 I would give ten percent of it to God. People thought I was crazy. One day I was writing out an institutional check. You may be thinking, *what's that?* Here's how it works. An institutional check is just like a real check, but it's actually not. You fill it out just like a check and then put it in the mailbox on the cellblock. The mail is then picked and taken to processing. When it gets to processing, the institution processes the "fake check," writes out a real check from money taken out of your account, and then the check is sent to wherever you want it to go. Every month I'd send a check to my grandmother. When my grandmother received the check, she'd then mail it to the ministry of my choice. I made sure every month my check was sent to a particular church because of my relationship with the pastor.

I remember filling out an institutional check one day, and my friend Bernard came up to me and said, "Why you sending your money to those people?" He was puzzled. My response, "I'm giving to God, and I won't be twice convicted of robbery." He walked away chuckling. Later on I heard through the grapevine that he was walking around calling me crazy. What was I doing? I was building. God was instilling within me a giving heart. As time progressed, I eventually moved up the success ladder in prison. I went from making $1.21 to $2.78, which is like the middle class! From $2.78 I eventually moved up to $3.78, which is like the upper middle class! You might be wondering, *Is there really a class system in prison?* Hecks yeah there is! All this time I could see God blessing me even in prison.

He had opened the door for me to make $3.78 as a legal aide. I even got a corner office with a brief case, a desk, and a typewriter. I was in the big leagues! What was I doing? Building! God had opened the door for me to reach the heights of financial success—in prison that is—and guess what? I continued to give and give and give. What was I doing? Building when everyone was laughing. Even now, I'm still building. My situation has changed, but one thing remains: I'm still a giver.

The reality is that God is calling all of us to build something. What will your response be? I'm sure Noah didn't get too excited when he found out that he was called to build a Titanic because he knew it meant work—120 years of work to be exact—but he never gave up. He kept building while everyone was laughing. There's a saying: "The same thing that makes you laugh will make you cry." Keep building when everyone is laughing because God is working in you to see that you become more and more like Him in character.

Myron Pierce

7 CLOSE CALLS

Prison can be a scary place. I had all kinds of misconceptions, objections, and ideas about what I thought it was like. As a result, it triggered all kinds of fears I didn't know I had. I think the most powerful form of fear is that of the unknown. Of course I knew what prison was like based on being in the juvenile prison, but I was sure that the prison I would go to would be quite different. It was the big house. In the big house are gang members, thieves, robbers, dope dealers, and killers. Who wouldn't be a bit fearful of what might happen to you? I was!

Bad things definitely happen to people in prison. I remember one time coming from work, and as I exited the doors to get to the prison yard, I saw about 10 guys beating a guy to a bloody pulp. The moment it started, prison guards were rushing to the scene. It was something like the movies in a way. What they did to that guy that day I would not wish on my worst enemy. With all of the blood I saw flowing from his head, it looked like they'd killed him. It's times like those in prison when the reality of where I was hit me like a ton of bricks. As I watched the prison guards tackle every one of those guys, I couldn't help but pray, "Lord, help me make it out of here alive."

One day I was on my way to work, and this guy came up to me and said, "Remember me?" Now, when someone asks that, there are really only two things that could have happened. Either you did something to them, or they did something to you. As he asked me that question, I couldn't help but think back to the previous days when this guy had just come to prison. I'd witnessed him staring at me, and I'd stare back because deep down he looked familiar. When people in prison looked familiar to me, I would almost never ask if I knew them or tell them they looked familiar because I didn't want to open up any worms from the past. But this was different; I had no choice. I could have said no, but it was time to deal with the situation. I must admit that when he came up to me and asked me that, I thought it was over; I was going to have to protect myself. I stayed calm and replied, "You look familiar." There was a long silence after that sentence. He looked down and then looked me straight in my eyes and said, "I'm the one who robbed you." My heart sank. It all came back to me. When I was selling marijuana on the streets, he was one of the guys who had connected with me to purchase some. He'd wanted to buy a large amount from me, so we set up the deal. I was to pick him up and then make the transaction. As I picked him up, he got in the car, and we took off to a disclosed location. What I didn't know was that he had a 9MM in his right hand. As I parked and looked to ask him if he had the money, he put the gun in my face and told me to give it up. At first I said nothing, completely stunned at what was happening. I refused to give him my drugs. After that he put the gun a bit closer to my head and said, "Nigga, you think I'm playing? I'll kill you." From there he took my marijuana, my money, my phone, and then jumped out of the car and ran. I was terrified! As he ran, still pointing the gun at me, I ducked, put the car in reverse, and floored it! As I floored it, he started shooting, and I somehow escaped. That day my life was spared. It was truly a close call!

After reliving the whole scene in my mind before this guy, I responded, "Yes, I remember you." The next thing that happened was nothing short of a miracle. Right after I said that, I said, "I forgive you." He looked at me with a dumbfounded look on his face. I went on to say, "If Jesus forgave me for all of the hurtful things I did to people, who am I to not forgive you? You are forgiven." I shook his hand and gave him the biggest hug that I could muster up. I could not believe I did that! I had never hugged a guy like that before in my life! The love of Jesus truly came upon me that day; I could literally feel the forgiveness of Jesus oozing through me as I walked away from our conversation. There's not a doubt in my mind that that situation could have gotten out of control, but because Christ was in my heart, it all worked out. The amazing thing about that close call is that before I left, that guy and I became great friends. On several occasions I got to share the gospel with him, pray with him, and invite him to our little church in prison. He would come to me and share his heart about how hard it was getting for him in prison. I was there for him in a way that honored God. There we were, two enemies, but reconciled unto each other because I'd been reconciled to Christ. Only God!

One time I was coming from work and noticed there was someone in my friend Scott's cell. Scott was a great brother and had just surrendered his life to Jesus. I looked into the room and saw two guys going through his belongings. Out of nowhere I yelled, "Hey, get out of there!" Out of me came this boldness, and they scurried out of there as fast as they could! After that I thought nothing of it because they didn't have time to take anything. A few days went by. On a Sunday right after worship service, a few brothers came up to me and said; "You know there's a hit out on you?" Those very guys were out to take my life. I looked at them and started laughing. They assured me that it was no laughing matter and that because I said something to the Hispanic guys who invaded Scott's room, they were going to get me. It turned out that the guys I yelled at were part of a Guatemalan gang and their leader wasn't too happy about me getting in their business. A level of fear gripped me.

That day I went to my jail cell and began to pray, "Lord, I was doing what was right; please protect me." One scripture came to my mind as I bowed my knee to Jesus, "When a man's ways please the Lord, He makes even his enemies to be at peace with him" (Prov. 16:7, NKJV). That was God's assurance to me that He had everything under control. From that point on, I squared my shoulders, trusted God, and claimed His promise of protection over me.

A few days passed, and I'd noticed that those two guys were no longer in population (meaning in the general population of the prison). I also noticed that the ringleader of the Guatemalan gang was nowhere in sight either. I didn't think much of it. I guess I thought they were maybe on room restriction in their cells. I mentioned previously that I was a legal aide in prison. Every Sunday I would help inmates who were in solitary confinement. Well, that night you would never believe who came walking in—those two guys and their ringleader! Somehow they were placed in solitary confinement. They walked in shackled and cuffed (as those in solitary confinement have to be.) They sat down, and I began to assist them in legal matters. There I was helping the very guys who sought to bring disaster to my life. God has a bit of a humor! Do you know what that did to those guys? It affected them drastically. One of the guys came back to get legal help the next week. That opened the door for me to talk to him about Jesus. He later revealed to me that he didn't even want to be in the gang, but that if he didn't do what he was told, he would be dealt with by the powers that be. Right there I was able to pray for him and assure him that Jesus loved him and was calling him to surrender his life. I don't think he ever did, but it was a great opportunity to share the love of Christ with him. I never had any problem out of those three again. The two guys were eventually released from solitary confinement, and the ringleader was placed on administrative confinement, which meant he was indefinitely restricted from going back to general population. Eventually he was sent to another prison. To this day I have no idea how they were taken to solitary confinement, but I do know that God made sure I was protected. There were many other close calls and situations in which my life was in danger, but through it all, not a hair on my head fell, not a bruise on my body, not a hurt inflicted on my being.

Stuff like that reminds me of Jesus while He was still on this earth. Out of all the good He was doing, all the miracles He performed, all the life-lifting words He spoke, people still sought to inflict injury on Him. In many instances, He was delivered. On several occasions He was able to finagle His way out. I love what He told a group of people, "No man takes my life, but I lay it down" (John 10:18). Jesus understood that regardless of all of the close calls He had, it mattered none. He was sent for a particular purpose, and no one was about to cause Him to deviate from His mission. That is what I love about serving God; regardless of the frustrations, temptations, and situations of discomfort, God will make sure that you not only survive but also thrive in the midst of close calls.

You can be assured that if God has a plan for your life—and He does—then it matters none what you face. There's a passage in the Book of Romans that says:

> What, then, shall we say in response to these tings? If God is for us, who can be against us.... Who shall separate us from the love of Christ? Shall trouble or hardship or persecution or famine or nakedness or danger or sword.... No, in all these things we are more than conquerors through him who loved us. For I am convinced that neither death nor life, neither angels nor demons, neither the present nor the future, nor any powers, neither height nor depth, nor anything else in all creation, will be able to separate us from the love of God that is in Christ Jesus our Lord. (Rom. 8:31,35, 37-39)

God doesn't promise us a safe ride, but He does promise us that in the midst of close calls He is there. I admit that there was much uncertainty for me in prison. There's a culture there that is in direct confrontation with the culture of Jesus. Every day I had to make decisions that were in conflict with the world of prison. However, it mattered none to me. I wanted to live for Jesus. I made up my mind before I stepped over the threshold of that prison that I would live for Him and that He would live through me.

I love what Paul the Apostle said in the Book of Acts,

> I consider my life worth nothing to me; my only aim is to finish the race and complete the task the Lord Jesus has given me—the task of testifying to the good news of God's grace. (20:24)

That's one of my favorite portions of scripture because it captures the attitude of my heart in prison then and even now. I am a prisoner of the Lord Jesus Christ. I fully know that life will not be perfect and that many more close calls await me, but I know God is with me. And He is with you.

He is for you regardless of the close calls.

8 STEPPING STONES

Have you ever heard someone say, "I'm a self-made man?" That's ridiculous! Now, I have a few soapboxes, so excuse me. I promise I won't reveal all of them. I'll preface this chapter by saying the reason I have a soapbox is simply to remind myself how much God really wants to cleanse me. All of that to say, soapboxes aren't wrong; it's how you use them that makes a world of a difference. So yes, I have a few of them. Okay, maybe more than just a few. One of them is this issue of independence. I'm not about to bash our country, but someone told me that any time you make a statement and say, "but," you cancel everything you previously said. Enough of the bunny trails.

I don't believe in independence. I think independence breed's rebellion. I won't deny that there is some kind of freedom that comes from independence, but what does it really produce? I'll give you a biblical example right out of the Bible. It's found in Genesis:

> The Lord God took the man and put him in the Garden of Eden to work it and take care of it. And the Lord God commanded the

man, "You are free to eat from any tree in the garden; but you must not eat from the tree of the knowledge of good and evil, for when you eat from it you will certainly die." (Genesis 2:15-17)

That seems like a pretty fair trade. Keep in mind that God created the first man, Adam, in His own image, blessed him, and freely pronounced the limitless potential over his life to be creative, demonstrative, and to reflect the glory of God. I have a question. What need did Adam have for independence? He was in a God-relationship that reflected the triune God. He lacked nothing. He had everything going for himself. In fact, God told him, "If you deviate from the way things are, you will surely die, Adam." Eventually God took a rib from Adam and then formed and fashioned woman (some say it like this, "Whoaaaaa man!").

Everything was great! Adam had an amazing job and an amazing wife. This healthy, thriving, and flourishing relationship existed vertically between the first couple individually with God and horizontally between each other. They experienced life dependent on God and interdependent of one another. Independence did not exist. They had no need for it. Now, if you recall the story, everything ended up drastically changing. Yes, the devil crept into the garden, deceived Eve into desiring the fruit, she gave it to her husband, and instantly they knew they were naked. What's the first thing they did?

> Then the eyes of both of them were opened, and they realized they **were naked**; so they sewed fig leaves together and made coverings for themselves. (Genesis 3:7, author's emphasis)

Did you see that? They disobeyed God and made a decision independent of Him. Their decision resulted in more decisions that led to complete abandonment from the plans of God, and ultimately, they *made coverings for themselves*. That sounds like independence to me. Eventually, Adam and Eve's independence gave way to a great distance between God and man.

On top of that, it perpetuated an unhealthy cycle of horrible relationships to the degree that the next horrendous episode in human history resulted in brothers engaged in conflict, which ended in a life lost. Cain killed Abel. Why? Independence. Cain saw no need for his brother, when in reality he needed him. We need each other. The sad reality is that some of us think we get to the top through independence, but we actually get there through interdependence.

This understanding of interdependence is what I call "stepping-stones." I remember walking out of church one day in prison, and God gave me a picture of a pond. In this pond were stones all in a row. They were like steps leading to the other side of the pond. God spoke to my heart and said, "Myron, those stones are the people whom I'm placing in your life to get you to the other side." After I heard that, I just wept. God was impressing on my heart that He would bring people into my life to help me get to where He wanted me to be. Feelings of joy overshadowed me! That day a trumpet went off in my heart. There I was in the most despicable place on earth besides the grave, and God was telling me that I was, number one, getting to the other side and, number two, that He was going to use people to help me. I wept.

This next page or two is dedicated to all of the people God has used in my life up to this point. Even before I knew He was at work, He was using people to draw me to Himself. This chapter could have easily been named "Numbers" or "Chronicles." I think it's that important to list as many people as I can. In so doing, it will become an encouragement to you that God is always at work in people's lives to see that you get to where He wants you to be. My prayer is that you would be blessed in reading it and begin to write your own list of people who God has used, is using, and will use to draw you closer to Him and His purposes.

Amillion Reed (my daughter). I was just a kid when her mother had her, but she's a sweet and amazing servant with potential to change the world, and I'm honored to call her my daughter!

Tanya Pierce (my mom). Myron Perry (my dad). Ruby Williams (my grandmother on my mom's side). Tranetta (my tattle-telling sister who was a blessing in my life in so many ways). Marcus (my aggravating brother who helped me grow tough skin). Tanisha and Unique (my baby sisters who taught me how to care for others by caring for them). Mr. Charlie (the bald-head, white guy who used to take me to children's church when I didn't even know it was church). Mr. McDuffy, who instilled a work ethic in me at a young age. All of my haters (I thought I might throw that in there. I love you. You meant it for harm, but God meant it for good). Ms. Houston (my elementary teacher who always smelled like cigarettes, but I knew she cared). James Pierce (my granddad who always seemed to help my mom out with bills). Claude Williams (my great-grandfather who always had a wise axiom to tell me). Aunt Naktangi (to this day she knows how to make me laugh and babysat me when I was a snotty nose little boy—and she loves Jesus!). Aunt Kathy (truly an amazing woman with fervor, faith, and extreme generosity in so many ways). Daisy (one of my first girlfriends; I'm so thankful she dumped me because I probably wouldn't have met my wife). My kindergarten teacher, Ms. Terry (she had the biggest smile and made me feel big when I looked so small). Maurtiez Ivy (my second mother, basketball coach, and mentor). OHA; thanks for giving us a place to stay in the projects. Kathy J. Trotter (she believed in me even when I was acting like a knuckle head. Clint McNeel (one of the godliest men I've ever met in prison). William Freeman (my brother from another mother; he and his family treated me like family when I had no money in prison). Brett Byford (he came to me when I was in prison; this guy lives what he believes), Tommy Taylor, Bev, Jack, Arlene, and everyone I've missed (some of the most amazing prison ministers in the world). Mother Valerie (she answered my phone calls when no one else did and embraced me as her son when I needed a mother). Kristin (I'll write about my amazing wife in a later chapter). Our whole Abide/Bridge Staff—Ron and Twany, Josh and Jen, Art and Isabel, Shawn and Jodi, Jeff and Bobbie Jo, Craig and Susan, Kainos and Sharon, Ron and Nicole, and all of the youth and interns (my spiritual family who has prayed, fasted, and loved me for me!)

I would not be where I am apart from the people I listed! There are so many people I did not list, but your crown is much more weightier than recognition in a book; your reward is in heaven! I'll end this chapter by highlighting a few people and how God used them as stepping-stones in my life to help me get to the other side. In light of them, I've been able to cross over to the other side. I'm going to summarize in one to two sentences who these people are and how they've impacted my life.

Morris Jackson took a chance on me and selected me to be a praise and worship leader in the life-learning dorm (a ministry ran by chaplains in jail) at the Douglas County Corrections Center. He saw that I had leadership potential and gave me an opportunity to serve.

Clint McNeel is doing life in prison but is probably one of the most dynamic missionaries in the world. I nicknamed him early on "The Simple Saint." He listened to me, prayed for me, mentored me, and most of all, was a dear brother commissioned by God to prepare men—including me!—for the mission field.

Tommy Taylor was a weekly preacher who came into the prisons faithfully. One of the greatest things I learned from him was to be a man of excellence. Most of all, he embraced me like a son and spoke words of destiny in the face of overwhelming odds that were stacked against me.

William Freeman became my second roommate in prison, which was totally a God-thing. In prison we became true brothers in the faith. We cried together, dreamed together, took communion together, argued together, believed God together, and served Jesus together. It was through "Free" that I learned the true definition of passion and love for God!

Brett Byford is one of the funniest guys you will ever meet. I first met Brett in 2003 when he, along with other Nebraska Football players, came in to be a blessing one night by speaking and preaching the Word. As he left the service that night, I slipped him a note and offered a few encouraging words. Shortly thereafter, he started visiting me weekly. We grew to be great friends! That relationship reflected what the scriptures teach, "As iron sharpens iron, so one person sharpens another" (Prov. 27:17, NIV).

My grandmother, Ruby Williams, is like my other mother (I know, I've adopted a lot of mothers!). She wrote to me faithfully, and I'm not just talking about a one-page letter; I'm talking a novel! I could always count on her to not only write me but to also answer my phone calls. She was a breath of fresh air in a toxic culture. She always reminded me of whose I was and who I was. Even before prison, before the gangs, crime, and jail time, she an example of a persevering woman who prayed for me fervently.

Even when she wasn't serving God and knew nothing about Jesus, she turned to me at the age of eight and said, "You and your brother are going to be preachers one day." I didn't even know what a preacher was, and I don't think she did either. Years later her prophecy came true!

Valerie Likely is my friend Curtis's mom. Again, she was like a mother. I can remember the countless telephone calls filled with tears and regrets. She'd simply remind me that God was building a résumé that He was using the prison experience to create in me a powerful man of God. She always told me, "Stay saved." In other words, stay "all in" at all times regardless of what happens. She prayed me through!

My Aunt Kathy is crazy, but I love her. She believed in my dreams when I didn't believe in myself. She went through the work to ultimately help me get into college and then showed up out of nowhere to be of assistance to me. I literally believe Jesus used her to get the ball rolling so that I could get on with my life and get a college education! I'll share about several other people in the last chapter, but I have one more person I must talk about: Cainos Manyara!

If you want to know what it means to be a radical world changer, you need look no further than Cainos. I mentioned him in the introduction of this book. This is a man who doesn't understand what it means to doubt. Cainos is a man of great faith. He jokingly has said in times past that walking hundreds of mile barefoot and through jungles just to get to school will create that kind of faith. Regardless of where he got the faith, he's a man who really believes that Jesus died for our sins, rose again, and is now seated at the right hand of the Father. He has taught me so much about the kingdom of God. But, the underlying theme of his life is the servant. Cainos is a servant of servants.

In the Bible Jesus is talking to His disciples about serving. He begins to wash Peter's feet, and Peter freaks out because he's ultra-sensitive to another man washing his feet. But Jesus intervenes and objects to Peter's insecurities and says, "Unless I wash you, you have no part with me" (John 13:8, NIV). Of course Peter goes overboard and is like, "Okay Jesus, do what you do and wash my hands, feet, and head." What I love about Jesus's last statement is that He clearly defines His followers as being servants, and He lands on this one statement:

> "Do you understand what I have done for you?" he asked them. "You call me 'Teacher' and 'Lord,' and rightly so, for that is what I am. Now that I, your Lord and Teacher, have washed your feet, you also should wash one another's feet. I have set you an example that you should do as I have done for you. Very truly I tell you, no servant is greater than his master, nor is a messenger greater than the one who sent him." (John 13:12-16)

When I read this scripture, it literally reminds me of Cainos. One day he called me and said, "I've got to come to your house." I instantly said, "Why?" He said, "I've got to wash your feet." In my mind I was thinking, *Okay, you've got to be kidding, I have corns, my feet stink, and this isn't normal.* But God reminded me of what Jesus did to His disciples. I reluctantly gave in, and he washed my feet. I still don't fully understand what motivated him to do such a gross thing apart from the sheer fact that he's radical. On the other hand, I learned something powerful. A servant is selfless. Cainos's selfless attitude has impacted thousands. I know he'd probably shun me even putting this much information about him in this book, but so what! Because this man of God has literally been used of God in such a way that I will never be the same. My prayer life is different, my giving, my faith life, and my devotion to Jesus have increased because I've seen a model of what it means to live for Jesus and like Jesus. Thank you, brother Cainos. Your life is worth imitating!

No one arrives a success independently. It takes helping people who have no agenda other than your kingdom success. Again, if I missed you, you know who you are. You've become the stepping-stones that God has used to launch me into this season of my life, and for that I am eternally grateful. Thank you!

9 Gold Nuggets

Most people in prison see their incarceration as a setback. From jump I viewed it as a setup for a comeback in life. I've learned that if you see obstacles, you will spend a greater amount of time and energy trying to remove them. On the other hand, if you see opportunities, you will have a greater chance of figuring out creative ways to leverage those opportunities for God's glory. Prison was an opportunity to overcome all of my mishaps and allow God to shape them into a bridge that I could cross over into His plans and purposes in this generation.

It's not about you. Life had become about me; I was not in a place in which I could be of any benefit to anyone. Prison taught me a harsh reality. When life is about you, you end up destroying and hurting everyone around you.

That was one of the first things I learned in prison: *it's not about me.* The moment I learned that became an opportunity for me to learn about Jesus. Life is about relationship with Christ and those in His family. It is about developing that incredible potential on the inside of every one of us.

It is about the mission of changing the world and touching the lives of all six billion people on the planet. The longer it takes us to see that life is not about us, the longer and more harmful we become to ourselves and others. Essentially, it is about Christ, God, Him. Scripture is clear: "In him we live and move and have our being" (Acts 17:28, NIV). When we understand that it's not about us, we are better and God can actually use us to change the world.

    I can remember being in my cell one night when I was in prayer and really struggling with the whole idea of my father, him not being in my life, and over thinking the fact that I was a product of parents who didn't practice safe sex. My father wasn't an integral part of my life. Even after committing my life to Christ, I still had rejection issues. When I was 16 I got caught in an argument with my dad over something, and I yelled at him and said, "You are not my dad!" In return he responded, "You are not my son!" That devastated me. Imagine a parent telling his or her kid that. In the course of time, my issues grew and God began doing a work in my life even after I'd become a Christian. One day the Lord directed me to a scripture: *"He chose us in him before the creation of the world to be holy and blameless in his sight…"* Ephesians 1:4 NIV. As I read it, the key word that God put on my heart was "chose." In that very moment, God spoke to me and said, "Because I chose you, it didn't matter how you got here." That set me free. I learned that regardless of how I got here, He chose. That means He had to think about it, and I was, in fact, on His mind. God chose me, and God chose you. For most of us, that's a hard pill to swallow. God has a way of speaking to us and getting through to us so that He can eventually shine through us.

    I was sitting in my cell one night, meditating and talking to God. I began to reflect on my life. It dawned on me that the situation I was currently in didn't make me bitter but it made me better, and that I would be leaving prison one day a different person. Paul says in the book of Romans that when we go through things it produces character, and the end result of character results in this hope we have. That all of a sudden eliminates the idea of being put to shame. I learned that as a result of prison I became better at knowing Christ, myself, and my calling. When you're in a situation, regardless of what it is, you have a choice to allow that situation to make you bitter or better, and those results will impact you and other people. Because of what I've gone through, whether I directly or indirectly made decisions that placed me in situations in which I had to undergo consequences, it made me better. Something that you can't pray away, you have to experience. Some situations we can't control, but we can control whether we get bitter or better. God wants us to know that the lessons we learn can help enhance our perspective on life, His kingdom, and ultimately result in bringing Him honor.

When I was in prison, I learned to embrace the pain. You may be thinking, *what is he talking about?* I can remember being in bed and thinking about the people I had hurt, and for a brief moment I was so pained by what I had done. It's kind of crazy, but I embraced it. I was there in the moment to feel it and be present in a way that the experience never left me. As a result, I am not the same. I am able to empathize with people more now. Prison was a painful place in a situation in which I wanted to leave but couldn't. Maybe for you it's a job or relationship(s). I've learned that when you embrace pain there is purpose in it because down the road there will be someone in the same situation, and because you've been there, you literally position yourself to give the same comfort. Embrace the pain. In so doing, I have a perspective when dealing with people and my own situations today.

There's something that happened to Jesus. He embraced pain on the cross for all of us. He suffered for us so that we might have life. What pain is God asking you to embrace? The apostle Paul embraced pain in his life, and people's lives were different because they saw the power of God at work in his life. They saw Christ. *"That I may know him, the power of his resurrection, and the fellowship of his sufferings… being conformed to his death"* Phil. 3:10-11 (NIV). Pain has a way of humbling us and causing us to look at the very character of Christ and to cry out for Him in desperation. Pain shows us not how strong we are but how frail we are. The thing about pain is that God is able to heal our pain. Because I was so present in my pain, God was right there to meet me in it. Did you know that you could be in pain, yet still experience the presence of God? The old hymn "There's Not a Friend Like the Lowly Jesus" by G.C. Hugg says:

"Jesus knows all about our struggles. He will guide till the day is done.   There's not a friend like the lowly Jesus. No, not one. No, not one."

What am I saying? The pain that you embrace will be the power that you walk in. Getting that revelation in prison allowed me to persevere even in the tears and doubts!

You've heard the old saying "You don't know what you've got until it's gone." It's so true. I went to prison and all of a sudden I started missing my freedom. Sometimes we take people, our freedoms, and our very lives for granted. When those things are taken from you, you miss them. What I've learned is that you can't take anything for granted. All of a sudden you sober up and see that what's gone is precious. I've learned to take time out to be thankful for the people in my life. I am so thankful for my wife. She sacrifices her time to love our sons and me. I'm thankful for the church that I get to co-pastor. What about after we die? For some of us, we're going to die without a relationship with Christ—not because it wasn't available but because we didn't choose it. It's now our opportune time to have a relationship with God through Jesus Christ. There is a place called heaven and a place called hell. And there are people in hell right now saying;

"I took for granted that that person told me about Jesus. I took for granted that that person shared with me that I could have eternal life to both be in heaven and have heaven."

We don't know what we've got until it's gone. I learned that principle in prison. I'm so thankful that after I die I won't be saying that I took Jesus Christ for granted. I won't be missing out on a relationship with Him because I have it now. Know what you've got. Know what's available, and value people. If you're that person who wants to have a relationship with God, His arms are wide open. You simply have to say, "I'm tired of living and running my own life. I've failed to comply with your standard of holiness. I've done all of that against you, God, and I turn from that and place my complete trust in Jesus Christ. I confess with my mouth and believe in my heart that Jesus was raised from the dead so that I might have life in the here and now. Amen."

Nothing is impossible to him who believes Mark 9:2 (NIV). Let that sink in. What people say is impossible is highly possible. It may look impossible that you'll ever come out of depression, low self-esteem, debt, or that your spouse will never change. They're not my words; they're God's.

There I sat in prison facing a long time, but I understood one thing: nothing is impossible. One of the scriptures in Hebrews 11 defines faith as the "substance of things hoped for and the evidence of things not yet seen." What is impossible in your life right now? I love what my mentor

Ron Dotzler says practically all the time, "Faith is nonsense." Faith is not something that you can see, taste, touch, feel, or hear. Faith is a God-given confidence. Faith is a God-given assurance.

I love what my friend Cainos said the other day to a group of high school students. He said, "Faith is inexhaustible." Just this morning at 4:30 a.m. a number of us gathered together for prayer and worship. During our time together, the Lord impressed upon our hearts to believe Him for one thing and to be in one accord. My good brother Ron Smith said, "Myron, what are we going to agree on?" My response, "That over the next seven days we might experience a mighty move of God marked by miracles, signs, and wonders." We all looked around in great expectation for what was about to happen. To wet our appetites for such a request, I had all of us turn to Acts 4:24, 30-31, which says:

> They raised their voices together in prayer to God.... Stretch out your hand to heal and perform signs and wonders through the name of your holy servant Jesus. After they prayed, the place where they were meeting was shaken. And they were all filled with the Holy Spirit and spoke the word of God boldly.

You would not believe what happened after that! After everyone had left, I stayed behind for a couple more hours. Around nine o'clock I went out of the doors of the church and saw someone who looked familiar. It was the daughter of a woman my dad used to date. I hadn't seen her for 11 years! We both locked eyes, completely shocked at this unplanned engagement. Come to find out, she had gone to prison, got addicted to crack cocaine, and lost everything including her kids. She had just left a job fair. Instantly I said, "I can take you home." As I pulled up at her house, she began to get out and asked me for a few dollars to get something to eat. I told her I didn't have any cash but then thought about the possibility of maybe having a gift card back at the office.

    I pulled up to the office and ran in to meet our business manger. All I needed was the McDonald's gift card that I thought we had. He looked in the safe, but there wasn't one. After that he pulled out a No Frills gift card and handed it to me. Just when I was about to walk out, he asked for the card back and then looked on the back of it and saw that there were only 11 cents on it. He took it from me and gave me a $25 gift card. Off we went to Wal-Mart, but while on the way, we decided to stop to see her mother. She hadn't seen me in years and was so surprised. After our short reunion, we went on our way. When we got to Wal-Mart, I told her that I would grab some items and that she could grab the items she needed. As I went to grab ground beef and hot dogs, my "sister" (not really my sister but the daughter of my dad's ex-girlfriend) was in another aisle grabbing items. As she was shopping, a woman turned to her and said, "Would you like a free coupon?" Bam! My stepsister said yes. She took the coupon and then thanked the woman. After that, the woman ended up giving her 15 to 20 more free coupons. Not money-saving coupons but free coupons. Eventually, we made it to the checkout line. Guess what? The groceries added up to $130! We walked in the store with a $25 gift card and left with $155 worth of groceries! Nothing is impossible! Friend, I want you to know that regardless of what you're facing, one thing I have learned is that nothing is impossible!

    As I bring this chapter in for a landing, I want you to know that God has many things to teach you and I about His kingdom. Fortunately, I was blessed to have an opportunity to go to prison. Prison became a platform for God to teach me "Gold Nuggets." I'm convinced that He wants you to uncover gold nuggets and that they are enough to transform your world!

10 Exit

For every entrance there's an exit. There's a time to leave where you are for the sake of where you're going. Before I go any further, I'd like to start this chapter off by giving you some good news. Earlier in the book I mentioned that my father wasn't a part of my life. But guess what? God allowed me to lead him into a relationship with Jesus! Today he became a Christ-follower! Today he asked Jesus to be Lord of his life! What a better way to start a chapter!

My dad called me on the phone today, and I actually missed it because I was on the other line. Right after I finished, I called him. We started chatting and shooting the breeze, and I asked him a question based on our last phone conversation. I said, "Dad, how's your healing going?" He has COPD (Chronic Obstructive Pulmonary Disease), and last week I prayed that Jesus would heal him. His response was very basic, "I'm good. Everything is fine." Then, I asked another question, "Dad, are you smoking cigarettes?" There was complete silence on the other end, and his response was, "Yes." He then went on to tell me that he was trying to stop, and I gently interrupted him and said that trying to stop smoking was a dead end leading to nowhere. I encouraged him to think in light of the fact that the nicotine has all of the control and that he doesn't, regardless of how many times he tries. The reality is that until we give up trying to control our lives and allow Christ to have the control, He can't come in and control what is controlling us. It seemed to click with him, and right after I said, "It's time to give your life to Christ." I was completely overjoyed, and I could hardly contain myself. Here was the man I barely knew growing up about to take the largest step he ever had taken in his life. I could barely hold it together as my father repeated after me, from his heart, the decision to follow Christ and to trust in full faith that He rose from the dead three days after His death, that we might be fully forgiven and freed to live for Him in power! If you're going to exit something, exit it like that. I think my dad's story is a great illustration of what it means to exit one place so that you might enter another.

Such it was with me. The law was changed, and it worked in my favor. (In short, I was ineligible for an early release from prison. The penal system calls this parole. The reason being, that I was on parole when I committed the crime that landed me in prison the second time. If a person commits a crime while on parole that person would not be given another chance at paroling). God was at work saving and healing people, and disciples were being raised up while I was in prison. Those were the joyous days where God was so much at work that even the guards would visit our small Bible studies to learn how they could live like Jesus or even have the faith to believe that He actually lived, suffered, died, and was resurrected on the third day that we might live a blameless and upright life.

How many of you know that it's not how you enter, but how you exit? I spent years in prison waiting for my exit strategy, seeking and searching how God was going to pull off the great miracle of transitioning me from the prison to the palace. With great favor and promotion, my case manager approved me to be considered for parole before 2018!

I remember standing before the parole board in 2006, and yes, they definitely had questions. It's practically normal for guys to stand before them with this Christian face about how they've changed, and then next thing you know, they are back in prison the next month; it happens. There I stood with Jesus, the only Advocate in the room at the time who was fully ready to present my case before parole board. The guards, caseworkers, and mangers had nothing but great things to say when it came to my release. However, one of the parole board members was very stern with me and gave me a clear warning that they'd heard many stories of transformation and were expecting my transformation to transfer into society and that I'd never be back. Little did they know, I'd been fully changed by Jesus and was ready to be sent to my city, Omaha, Nebraska.

I'd been granted parole by the state of Nebraska! Feelings of joy, assurance, and confidence showered me! I left that parole hearing fully on fire! I can remember it like it was yesterday, leaving that room, screaming at the top of my lungs, "I told you! I told you!" The very people who doubted me were speechless. The very people who doubted that what God told me in secret would actually happen. I just want to take this time to tell you to never doubt what God tells you in private at the expense of people who don't get the same word. If I've learned anything up to this point, it is: "what is most impossible is most possible." That's what being outrageous is all about. It's about looking at the worst situation and seeing something different!

Abraham is a great picture of what it means to be outrageous. I said earlier that *outrageous* means, "to exceed the limits of what is usual." Abraham is the epitome of a man who faced great odds, but "outrageous" marked his life. It mattered little to him that he couldn't have kids. It mattered little to him that he was an old guy and that when everyone was beckoning him to throw in the towel, he refused to do so. The scripture says about him:

> Therefore, the promise comes by faith, so that it may be by grace and may be guaranteed to all Abraham's offspring—not only to those who are of the law but also to those who have the faith of

> Abraham. He is the father of us all. As it is written: "I have made you a father of many nations." He is our father in the sight of God, in whom he believed—the God who gives life to the dead and calls into being things that were not. Against all hope, Abraham in hope believed and so became the father of many nations, just as it had been said to him, "So shall your offspring be." Without weakening in his faith, he faced the fact that his body was as good as dead—since he was about a hundred years old—and that Sarah's womb was also dead. Yet he did not waver through unbelief regarding the promise of God, but was strengthened in his faith and gave glory to God, being fully persuaded that God had power to do what he had promised. (Rom. 4:16-21)

Talk about a story! Even though Abraham's situation wasn't ideal, he didn't weaken in his faith. I can relate to Abraham because his story is my story, only in a different format. Were there times of uncertainty or doubt regarding what God had told me about being released? Sure! I'm still human, but the truest thing about me wasn't my doubt or my fears but rather me considering the promise God had made me that I would exit prison because of the calling He had on my life. I got stronger as the days grew longer. I meditated on the promise! I thought, talked, and believed and was "fully persuaded that God had power to do what He had promised." That is outrageous faith!

I don't know what you are facing right now and that really doesn't matter. What matters is that you are called by God to exit a purposeless cause and enter into a powerful calling. Will you make a decision to see yourself exiting that place of barrenness? I don't care how long it takes. If you can believe now by faith that you are outrageous and that you can exceed and supersede the expectations and opinions of men, and even yourself, and embrace a life that is rich in quantity and quality, then you can exit in order to enter into a land flowing with milk and honey—a land flowing with an abundance of provision! Today is your day to exit just as I exited prison!

11 Transition

God has a way of making your wildest dreams come true. Although I had been granted release from prison, it was actually just the beginning of the process. Being granted release means that I had to walk out an 18-month process of transitioning from medium maximum security prison to community custody security prison, which ultimately meant that I still had a little bit of time to do before actually getting out. The good thing is that I wasn't going to have to do the remainder of my time in the Lincoln Correctional Center. Once a person is granted parole, he or she must begin the process of transitioning out systematically. For me, that meant I would ultimately be sent to the Community Correctional Center in Omaha (CCC-O). That move afforded me an opportunity to "be out of prison, but not out of prison." Every person who goes to CCC-O has the chance to work a real job and/or go to college while they await release.

Early on in prison, I'd decided that I would, in fact, try to go to Bible school, so that I did. As I transitioned to CCC-O, I'd already submitted my application to Grace University for entry into their school. That process took quite a long time— something I was used to, though, being in prison. Come to find out, Grace's faculty had gone into deliberation to decide whether or not they should let me in. That was probably the longest wait in my life—apart from that of waiting to get sentenced to 14 to 30 years in prison. I'd been adamant about getting into Grace University because the stars were lining up, and God was definitely placing people in my path to make it happen. To name a few, the champion in helping me get into Grace was my aunt Kathy. It's interesting how God places people in your life at the right place, at the right time. A few months prior to me actually applying to Grace, my aunt had begun writing me. It turned out to be a blessing because she provided me the encouragement and hope that maybe it was the will of God that I get into college.

After much prayer and patience, I received what I was looking for: entry into Grace University! Have you ever felt like you were so in the will of God that it seemed like a dream? As I read that letter, feelings of accomplishment and great gain paraded the streets of my heart. I got accepted! With great gain comes great challenges! Paul the Apostle understood that well in 2 Corinthians 12:7-10 (NIV):

To keep me from becoming conceited because of the surpassingly great revelations, there was given me a thorn in my flesh, a messenger of Satan, to torment me. Three times I pleased with the Lord to take it away from me. But he said to me, my grace is sufficient for you, for my power is made perfect in weakness. Therefore I will boast all the more gladly about my weaknesses, so that Christ's power may rest on me. That is why, for Christ's sake, I delight in weaknesses, in insults, in hardships, in persecutions, in difficulties, for when I am weak, then I am strong.

In this particular case, Paul tried his best to pray away the challenges, but God had another route in mind. God's solution for Paul's thorn was *grace*. The thing that resonates with me is the last sentence of the passage, "I delight in weaknesses, in insults, in hardships, in persecutions, in difficulties..." I get that! I get it that when challenges occur they are simply opportunities for God to show up. If we're honest, we don't fully yield to that frame of reference all the time.

In my case, I'd been accepted into Grace University, but the *difficulty* was that I didn't have all of the resources to go to school my first year. According to the law, federal funding is prohibited for any prisoner in the penal system. Now, place yourself in my shoes:

- Given a Jeremiah 29:11-promise
- Tentative release date of 2018 overturned
- Favor all throughout my prison sentence
- Never lacked while I was in prison
- Won many people to Jesus in prison
- Entrance into Grace University
  Do you see how it would stump you to get that far and even get accepted into Grace, but not have all of the funding? I admit that it set

me back mentally. So much doubt reigned when I got that news that I had to harness all of it and go back to what I knew to do in difficult situations: pray! And that I did! I prayed until I got an answer!

Because of the graciousness of Grace University, they were able, as well as the state, to offer me a few scholarships. And then another source came in all in one month! However, I was still short one whole semester! How would God fix this? How would the God who is more than enough provide for me? Through an unlikely source! Clint McNeel.

I mentioned Clint many chapters ago. I nicknamed him the "Simple Saint" when I first met him because he'd always say, "Myron, I'm just a simple man." I never understood that phrase until the end of my prison sentence. It's the simple people who change the world. Simple people understand that it's not about them, but Him. Simple people understand that they are missionaries in a culture that is in need of King Jesus. Finally, simple people are readily accessible to being used of God in small and/or great ways!

Somehow, Clint found out that I was short on tuition. Right before it was time for me to start my first semester in college, I received a $5,000 check from him. I was flabbergasted, astounded, and amazed! I had no clue that he was packing that kind of cash! One more thing about a simple person: boasting in themselves is prohibited! To this day, I'm taken aback on how faithful God is!

Eventually, I started school at Grace University with my whole first year taken care of financially. The faculty loved me, took care of me, and accepted me as their own.

I had so much fun during my first year at Grace University. I even ran for President of my class. Guess what? I won! The first black president of a freshman class at Grace University! I'm a pioneer! Sorry, no boasting, right?

Even though, at the time, I was still incarcerated in community custody prison, I was having the time of my life going to Grace. I even landed a job at Grace as a janitor, so I was able to store up some cash to save before my release. I was the best Janitor at Grace University. You have to remember one thing: my first job in prison was working in the kitchen, and my second a janitor on the cellblock; this was easy money! I did it to the best of my ability. I nicknamed myself "Pastor of the Toilets"! I made it my aim to make sure people experienced the cleanest toilets in Omaha, Nebraska. Why did I have that attitude? Because I knew that I wouldn't be cleaning toilets forever. I understood one thing: I was in transition!

I wonder what would have happened if the people of Israel would have understood that leaving Egypt and entering the wilderness was transition. The wilderness was simply the "land between." They would not have been there for long. Think about it: an 11-day trip took 40 years. That is ridiculous! What did I learn transitioning from medium maximum-security prison to community security prison to Grace University? Learn all you can in transition and keep your eyes on the promise. There's one promise that I kept in transition:

> "For I know the plans I have for you," declares the Lord, "plans to prosper you and not to harm you, plans to give you hope and a future." (Jer. 29:11)

There are an innumerable amount of promises laid up for you, that if apprehended by faith will result in an *outrageous* life! How bad do you want outrageous? Do you really want to exceed the limits of usual? My question for you is: how far will you go? What are you willing to lose to gain it all? Let me give you insight into an outrageous statement made by one of the greatest men in history:

> What is more, I consider everything a loss because of the surpassing worth of knowing Christ Jesus my Lord, for whose sake I have lost all things. I consider them garbage that I may gain Christ. And be found in him, not having a righteousness of my own that comes from the law, but that which is through faith in Christ-the righteousness that comes from God on the basis of faith. I want to know Christ-yes, to know the power of his resurrection and participation in his sufferings, becoming like him in his death…" (Phil. 3:8-10 NIV)

The beginning of an outrageous life, wherever you are in life—in transition or fully in the plans of God—begins with really knowing Christ! Almost all of the Israelites died in transition (the wilderness) because they failed to, by faith, trust in the One who was able to deliver on His promises. May that not be you. May it be said of you that you dove head first into a full knowledge of whom Christ is and what He wants to do in your life. It's your season, my friend. "Usual" does not have to take up residence in your life. Our culture is doing the usual thing—life without Christ. Do you want to experience the limit-breaking power of God? Do you want a solid foundation whereby you can stand in the midst of any story? Then, Christ is the *outrageous* cornerstone on which you can build your life.

12 The Land of Promise

One mantra that I've been using lately is: "This is not the ceiling; it's only the baseline." I think the challenge of success is figuring out a way to celebrate your successes while still looking outward in the future with an attitude of "God isn't done." Such was my challenge. Things were going well at Grace University: I was making great grades, meeting new people, working, and setting in order all of my ducks in preparation for my release. Things couldn't possibly get better, right? Wrong! Things got greater!

While at Grace, every student must find a place of ministry to serve alongside of; it's called servant leadership training. Every year my school would have a ministry fair. All of the ministries from Omaha would come for a day, set up their booths, and try to attract as many college students as possible. I can still remember the first fair I went to; there were so many ministries to choose from. My dilemma was: considering my long history of run-ins with the law and prison, would any ministry even allow me to serve? This was pretty scary for me because I didn't want to be judged based on my past but rather on what God was presently doing in and through me. I persevered, trusted God, and made my rounds to the different ministry booths, making small talk but not going too deep into whom I was. I basically perused my way around the ministry fair secretly hoping that there was a ministry that would accept me for me and totally embrace me. Finally I found a ministry that I felt really good about: Compass Ministries! I stopped at the booth, picked up an information card, and began to read it. It was located just three blocks from my old neighborhood. In fact, three blocks from where I was born—3335 Lafayette! This had to be the place God was calling me to serve. After asking a few short questions, the lady representing Compass was ready to sign me up!

A week later I showed up ready to serve. I didn't even care what kind of ministry I served in as long as I got to serve. Christ has a way of doing that to you. When you've been genuinely changed, you'll serve anywhere. I was read to scrub toilets, vacuum, or hold the door. Whatever I could do to serve. I found out shortly thereafter that Compass was affiliated with Christ Community Church and that this faith-based organization's sole purpose was to minister to children and youth in such a way that they become transformational indigenous leaders. I jumped on an opportunity like that!

My primary role at Compass was to simply be a Fun Volunteer. Every Sunday afternoon I'd arrive early to get my instructions from the super, amazing Stacie Anderson. She'd lay out what she wanted me to do, whether it was facilitate a small group discussion, dress up as an Old Testament figure, or dance during praise and worship! We had hilarious times! Most of all, I was in my element. To be back in the same community serving kids who were from broken homes and bruised pasts did something to me; it energized me. All my years of bad decisions and horrible circumstances were building for me not only a testimony but also a résumé to draw from.

Paul the Apostle said in 2 Corinthians 1:3-7 NIV

Praise be to the God and Father of our Lord Jesus Christ, the Father of compassion and the God of all comfort, who comforts us in all our troubles, so that we can comfort those in any trouble with the comfort we ourselves have received from God. For just as the sufferings of Christ flow over into our lives, so also through Christ our comfort overflows. If we are distressed, it is for your comfort and salvation; if we are comforted, it is for your comfort, which produces in you patient endurance of the same sufferings we suffer. And our hope for you is firm, because we know that just as you share in our sufferings, so also you share in our comfort.

There's something about being able to relate to people. Serving those children at Compass put me in touch with their weaknesses. I was able to understand where they were coming from because I was once there. I heard someone once say; "Until you've walked a mile in my shoes you can't possibly understand my pain." In a sense that is so true!

I served at Compass for many months. One day I went and noticed a new girl coming every Sunday with two little Black kids. I actually thought it was pretty noble and sincere that this young lady was spending her time investing in kids. Little did I know that the young lady I thought was noble actually had other motives! Right! She was there to check me out. Come to find out, Stacie Anderson, the children's director at the time, had told this young lady, Kristin, about me. Yes! She'd given Kristin all of the information on me, about me, and so forth. They actually had gone on Myspace (a social network) to look at my profile. That led to Kristin (who had previously done an internship through University of Nebraska-Lincoln) going to see me.

Sometimes it takes guys a little longer to get the hint when a young lady is checking them out. Stacie had done her job; she'd gotten Kristin to go to Compass. Now God had to work on my heart to help me see that the woman of my dreams was going to Compass every week to serve. To make matters worse, around that same time I'd been praying through the whole wife thing, and I'd come to one conclusion and actually prayed, "God, I'm not going to date. I'm going to keep my eyes solely focused on you. So, no dating. Amen!" Word to the wise: never tell God what you're not going to do because He laughs at stuff like that.

Eventually, Kristin and I ended up talking! A rather interesting event happened that caused our two worlds to cross. Out of all things, a carnival. That's right! Compass ministry put on a carnival for the children, and Kristin simply asked me, "Can I paint your face?" What a way to capture a guy's heart, right? One thing led to another, and Kristin ended up taking me back to the work release center where I resided awaiting release from prison.

That one ride home turned into her picking me up for school, and that picking me up for school resulted in me asking her one question, "Can we date?" My side of the story (and I'm not changing it) is that Kristin turned me down the first time I asked her. *I* recall her saying no. Her side of the story is that she simply didn't want to go too fast. Regardless of whose side you believe, we eventually ended up dating.

It wasn't long until Kristin started telling me about a man named Ron Dotzler, and how it was important that I meet him because of his heart for the inner city of Omaha. If there's one thing about Kristin I've learned over the years: if she insists on something, you'd better check into it. I began to ask more questions about this Ron Dotzler guy. Eventually Kristin set up a time for him and I to meet. I remember it like it was yesterday. Ron and I met on my school's campus. At the time, I'd just started going to Grace University. We introduced ourselves and off Ron went asking many, many questions about me, my life, my story, and how I came to know the Lord. In turn, he began unfolding the story of his life, how he'd come to know the Lord, and how for over 20 years he'd tirelessly worked in the inner city of Omaha. By the end of the meeting, he'd invited me to speak at the last church he and his wife planted: Bridge Church.

A couple of weeks later, I shared my story at Bridge Church; it was an amazing time. I'd been attending another church and had no intentions on even considering a church move. But God had another thing in mind. It wasn't long until Ron wanted to meet with me again. This time, the meeting was about me joining Abide Network (the revitalization organization that he'd started) and Bridge Church. I immediately accepted the offer to join the effort of revitalizing North Omaha. My role at Bridge Church at the time was to lead the freshly new youth ministry. It was an exciting time of serving at Abide Network and Bridge Church!

I went on staff at Abide Network and Bridge Church around May of 2008, and shortly thereafter I was released from prison in August of 2008. In that same year, I got engaged, and 12 months later I was married to Kristin Petersen on May 17, 2009! God had been faithful to save me, preserve me, bless me to go to Grace University, connect me with my wife,

Kristin, and grace me to connect with an awesome ministry in North Omaha!

To date, I am currently on the Core Leadership Team of Abide Network as Program Director for Youth and Families and Co-Pastor of Bridge Church. I've had an amazing time co-leading with my friend Josh Dotzler (former Creighton basketball player.) In fact, him and I often say, "Who would have ever thought an ex-convict and an ex-Creighton basketball player would be leading a church together?" Along with my amazing friend Josh comes an amazing staff team that makes what we do fun, exhilarating, and amazing: Twany Dotzler (Ron's wife); Shawn Deane (our business manager—not to mention that he always hounds me about receipts); Bobbie Jo (who held me responsible for finishing this book); all of our young leaders: Myhiah, Janesha, Anahi, Tim, and Jeremiah; Craig (our partnership coordinator); Isabel (an amazing woman of God); and finally, Becky (one person you don't want to mess with—a no-nonsense worker who loves Jesus).

Here I am almost three years into marriage and almost four years into ministry, and I love it. To date, I've led hundreds to Jesus, preached to thousands, seen many people healed, gang members in love with Jesus, businessmen surrendered to God's call, and a city in the process of looking more and more like heaven. The work isn't finished, but I'm convinced that the more *outrageous* you and I become, the more transformed we become,

and that results in a changed world!

ABOUT THE AUTHOR

Myron Pierce is a graduate of Grace University where he obtained a Bachelor's Degree in Biblical Studies and Business Leadership. He is married to Kristin and together they have two sons Jericho and Judah. Myron also has a daughter named Amillion. Myron and Kristin live in Colorado Springs, Colorado where they are currently launching a new church called Passion City Church a church that emphatically seeks to "reach people who are far from Christ and lead them into a radical life change."

Made in the USA
San Bernardino, CA
30 January 2013